THIS BOOK IS GENEROUSLY SPONSORED BY:

CHASE

1STBANK

usbank

WELLS FARGO

The Persistence of VISION

The Denver Metro Chamber of Commerce

By Fred Brown

FG
FULCRUM
GROUP
Golden, Colorado

Library of Congress Cataloging-in-Publication Data
Brown, Fred, 1940-
The persistence of vision : the Denver Metro Chamber of Commerce / by Fred Brown. -- 1st ed.
p. cm.
Includes bibliographical references.
ISBN 1-56373-190-8 (978-1-56373-190-7)
1. Denver Metro Chamber of Commerce--History. 2. Denver Metropolitan Area (Colo.)--Commerce. 3. Business enterprises--Colorado--Denver Metropolitan Area. 4. Denver Metropolitan Area (Colo.)--Economic conditions. I. Title.
HF5047.B76 2011
381.06'078883--dc22
2011005677

Printed in the United States of America by Malloy Incorporated
0 9 8 7 6 5 4 3 2 1

Design by Patty Maher

Fulcrum Group
4690 Table Mountain Drive, Suite 100
Golden, Colorado 80403
800-992-2908 • 303-277-1623

Dedication

This book is dedicated to Joe Blake, president and CEO of the Denver Metro Chamber of Commerce from 1999 to 2009, and current chancellor of the Colorado State University System. For his leadership and friendship, we are grateful for all he has done and who he is.

—The Board and Staff,
Denver Metro Chamber of Commerce

Throughout this book, leaders and laureates have reminisced over a century of extraordinary actions and achievements that occurred through the Denver Metro Chamber of Commerce and the organization's continual and focused business leadership.

Woven together, these achievements illustrate the backdrop of the Colorado we love. Yet, it is important to note that these actions did not occur without extraordinary sacrifice, commitment, resources and a unwavering focus on the territory ahead and a clear vision for what we want this state to be; a place we proudly call home.

From the Chamber's early days as the Board of Trade when its leaders quickly raised the financial resources required to ensure the Queen City of the Plains was not left behind as economic prosperity rode the rails, to recent actions like the defeat of statewide ballot measures Amendments 60, 61 and Proposition 101, the business community, through the Chamber's leadership, has had a strong and unwavering voice focused on the betterment of Colorado. For that, we should all be proud.

—*Joe Blake*

Contents

Acknowledgments

Originally, this was going to be a book about Denver International Airport and how the Denver Metro Chamber of Commerce and its various committees and affiliated organizations played major roles in winning popular approval for the massive project. Joe Blake, the former chamber president and CEO, and M. Doak Jacoway, the chamber's chairman as the twentieth century ended and the twenty-first began, were the instigators of the effort, involved from its beginning in 2007.

With additional input from a steering committee, the original concept grew into a broader goal: a book that would go more into the history of the chamber, its public-private partnerships with state and local governments in a series of projects that had to be approved by voters, and the politics involved in making these changes happen. So it became a primer of sorts on how to win public support for any number of infrastructure improvements that are crucial to the region's economic health, but require the investment of tax dollars—always a tough sell.

In addition to Jacoway and Blake's efforts, initial financial support was provided by a number of local community leaders, including Don Kortz, Tom Honig, Doug Jones, and Dick Robinson. Kate Horle, the Denver Metro Chamber's director of communications and marketing, kept everyone headed in more or less the same direction. The author, who began this endeavor thinking he was going to be only a ghost writer, thanks them all for their input, support, and counsel.

Denver, 1860

From a sketch by Co . D. H. Huyept, published in *Leslie's Weekly*, December 15, 1860. Photo courtesy of the Denver Public Library Western History Collection, Z-4046.

Chapter 1

The Persistence of Vision

Despite its many attractions, Colorado never has been an overconfident kind of place. The state and Denver, the booming city at its heart, always have been anxious about their place in the world, worried about, being left behind, yet eager to get things done and anxious to continue moving forward. Like most places, the community at the foot of the Rocky Mountains has had its ups and downs, good times and bad, but over the years it has developed ways to bring about major civic improvements. That positive development makes the Denver area different from some other regions that haven't fared as well over the years. And in every one of these successes, the business community—not just in Denver, but across the region—has played a leading role.

Imagine a Great City was the campaign slogan for former Denver mayor Federico Peña when he ran for his first four-year term in 1983. The story goes that his campaign staff originally thought the pitch was, well, maybe just a bit of a stretch, a little vague and grandiose. But as time has shown, it nicely describes where the city and region believe they are today. "I think we're

Panning for gold in the placer mining district of (possibly) Clear Creek, circa 1890–1910. Photo courtesy of the Denver Public Library Western History Collection, L. C. McClure MCC-1918A.

Denver Chamber of Commerce building at Fourteenth and Lawrence, from 1890 to 1900. Photo courtesy of the Denver Public Library Western History Collection, X-18431.

there," said Tom Clark, executive vice president of the Denver Metro Chamber of Commerce. "We really have come to a world-city place."

A substantial reason for that is the sense of regionalism that has developed in this isolated metropolis—the notion that big things can't be done unless the business and political communities work together instead of constantly competing. There's something to be said for being a long way from other big cities; it fosters a need to be self-reliant and a sense of being different, but in a good way. Coloradans can be defensive when criticized, but they're very proud of what they've accomplished.

Sometimes it seems that Denver gets a disproportionate amount of attention for a metropolitan area with fewer than 3 million inhabitants. It sits in the middle of the least-populous time zone, the one that never gets mentioned in television promotional announcements. It may be the loneliest outpost in flyover land, with no other major urban area within more than 500 miles. And yet it seems to account for more than its fair share of news media ink and airtime, nationally and even internationally.

There are good reasons for this attention. One is obviously the physical setting. People up and down the Front Range can look to the west every day and be inspired by majestic 14,000-foot peaks—mountains, ironically, that were an early barrier to development. Mountains provide a populist, democratic sort of majesty—much more accessible to the eye and the other senses than the coastlines at either end of the continent.

Civic pride, and the striving to justify that sense of being special, always have been part of the economic equation. In the last years of the twentieth century and the first years of the twenty-first century, the region, and Denver especially, compiled an impressive list of achievements. New public facilities for culture and sport were built, along with high-end private developments and an extensive transportation system, including an increasingly popular light-rail system. At the top of the list, for its political and economic impact, is Denver International Airport (DIA), one of the largest airports in the world, with almost limitless potential for expansion. As a run-up to this incredible spurt, the region was almost forced to develop an enviable spirit of regional cooperation.

This book is a look at Colorado's and the Denver area's history of striving, a history of many achievements and the occasional failure. It is also a prognosis on where the region might go in the future. And it is intended to serve as a primer for future leaders who might learn from the successes of recent leadership.

Ups and Downs

Colorado's history is not unique: every region has its cycles of booms and occasional busts. Founded in the days of a restless search for precious metals, Denver saw its earliest boom softly fizzle in a post-gold-rush period of doldrums. Later, the recession of the 1930s gave way to explosive growth in the days after World War II. A grinding downturn in the area's economy in the 1990s followed the heady days of natural resources development in the 1980s. That latest uptick was timely and fortunate. An infusion of public works projects played a major role in bringing the region out of that economic low, and none of those stimulating projects would have happened without the ambition of the business community and the support of the public. The effect has had staying power; the new infrastructure has helped the region weather the global economic meltdown that struck in late 2008 and early 2009. The impact in Denver and the Rocky Mountain region has not been as severe as it has been elsewhere.

Government, including the relocation of some major federal offices to Colorado in the postwar years, has for a long time played a role in Colorado's economic stability. But it hasn't been handouts so much as it has been opportunities. The government's role in Colorado is more partnership than paternalism. The region's basic Western spirit of independence is reflected in its politics—restlessly bipartisan—and in its citizens' generally tolerant disposition toward change and toward others. Its populace is better educated than most, is younger, famously fitter, more devoted to outdoor activities, and, certainly not least on this list, more willing to approve spending money on visionary projects.

Coloradans vote on things. They've grown accustomed to it. The Colorado General Assembly is the only legislature in the country that can't raise taxes without specific voter approval. That unique restriction, which applies also to revenue increases, has led to some peculiar policy difficulties. But Colorado voters are generous, and discerning, in approving projects, taxes, and policy changes that improve what is already one of the most pleasant and vibrant environments to be found anywhere.

In the 1990s, the region raced through a decade of new and improved public facilities worth about $10 billion total. All of them were approved by voters, even when they didn't need to be. They included cultural facilities, baseball and football stadiums, wider freeways and more light-rail transit, and bonds for all manner of repairs and additions. The largest of these—representing half the total, at $5 billion—was DIA. And, sitting in his chamber office, former Denver Metro Chamber president and CEO Joe Blake said, "This idea of building an airport really was hatched in this place here." The airport project was the compelling reason behind the Greater Denver Corporation, spawned as a stimulus to get the region out of a terrible recession.

DIA is "the perfect example" of a project backed by government and business that had "a long-term, game-changing impact," said Kelly J. Brough, who succeeded Blake as chamber president and CEO in 2009. It goes beyond the immediate stimulus of creating jobs to establish a presence that will foster prosperity for decades to come, Brough said. It was, she added, "the smartest, most critical economic decision Mayor Peña and business leaders made years ago."

Projects like DIA are examples of how the Denver Metro Chamber is not as hard-wired conservative as some might expect. It more often works with government than against it. Former Colorado governor Bill Owens, a Republican, has joined with the chamber to support several ballot issues. He's not shy about saying that "the chamber does seem to have a predisposition toward spending initiatives." Whether it's new infrastructure projects or a change in fiscal policy, the chamber and its members are not averse to increasing the inflow of government revenue, as long as it's for a good purpose. Progressive? More like "pragmatic," said Tamra Ward, the chamber's senior vice president for public affairs and communications. *Progressive* lately has taken on a more left-leaning meaning than it once had, and that certainly does not describe the chamber. It supports government "investment" more than "stimulus," Brough said, "a long-term foundational shift in terms of future economic growth"—jobs now, jobs later.

Political personalities inevitably are in the spotlight as these public projects come to fruition. Elected officials provide the administrative leadership and the bully pulpit to bring them to reality. But it's typically the business community that had planted the seeds of the idea, and it's the business community that continues to provide support when the inevitable criticism surfaces. "Really courageous businesspeople make really courageous decisions...even under withering media attack," Tom Clark said.

The need to vote on pretty much everything in Colorado means the public must be convinced to endorse the ambitions of its leaders, public and private. Early public involvement creates the political foundation for eventual widespread support. And, of course, developing that support also requires money. In virtually every one of the projects built in the Denver region over the decade of the 1990s and beyond, the business community was involved from the beginning. And when it came time to vote, businesses provided money and people-power for the ballot-issue campaigns.

Working Together

Denver's history of local business and local government working together traces back to the city's ramshackle beginnings on the banks of Cherry Creek. It's a challenging environment down there in the bottoms; when it's not muddy, it's dusty. The temperature can plummet and soar through forty or fifty degrees in a single day. The sun bakes, the wind whistles, and sometimes it gets bone-cracking cold. As in much of the West, the region's earliest European wanderers were explorers, then trappers and traders. It took a hardy breed to deal with the often bold geography and fickle weather. But until flickering rumors of gold and other precious metals began sweeping the country in the middle of the nineteenth century, there really wasn't much to draw people to the foot of the Rockies. When the city was founded in the late 1850s, its survival was by no means assured. It sits at the edge of the high, arid, and empty plains that stretch to the east. The towering mountains to its west were a formidable obstacle. If it were to have any hope of surviving, let alone thriving, it needed two critical things: a reliable supply of water, and transportation access to the rest of the country.

M. Doak Jacoway, a former chairman of the Denver Metro Chamber of Commerce board of directors, credits three local leaders in particular with establishing the foundations that the region today takes for granted, but without which there would be no Denver as we know it. Walter S. Cheesman brought reservoirs and water treatment to the young city in the 1890s. He was a visionary, but he also was a businessman who turned the business of supplying water into a personal fortune. Mayor Robert W. Speer led the efforts for city planning and parks, and his legacy is celebrated by the parkway that bears his name. Mayor Benjamin F. Stapleton in 1922 embraced air travel and in 1929 dedicated the airport that later bore his name—an airport that eventually outgrew itself and was replaced in a massive, and sometimes controversial, community redevelopment project.

A large part of this book is devoted to the campaign that led to the building of that new airport, from the false starts and the failed technologies to what even its critics concede is one of the most passenger-friendly airports in the world. At one point, nearly everyone favored expanding the existing Stapleton airport onto the Rocky Mountain Arsenal. The land was heavily contaminated from years of chemical weapons and fertilizer manufacturing, but it was available. The military and industrial owners and contractors were abandoning the site, and one runway already had been extended onto Arsenal land. Most agreed Stapleton couldn't grow without that expansion, and moving aircraft operations farther north seemed like a good way to deal with the airport's unhappy neighbors to the west and north, who had sued over noise pollution.

Everyone was in favor of Arsenal expansion, that is, with one important exception: Adams County, where the new airport facilities would have to be built, was adamantly opposed because of noise and safety questions. The county's opposition forced airport supporters to look elsewhere. That's when Denver got into one of the most heated arguments of its civic life.

How those arguments were addressed, and how the controversy continued for months, even years, after the opening of the airport, provide some important lessons that apply to other issues and infrastructure as well. "I would argue very strongly that it was the airport that was the first major demonstration that we as a metro community can actually work together," said former Denver mayor Federico Peña, whose demonstrated abilities in handling that project won him an appointment as secretary of transportation after he left the city office.

Now it's hard to find a credible critic of the airport. After DIA opened on February 28, 1995, there was an early period of buyers' remorse, when airfares were high and questions were raised about the airport's survival. But now the prevailing attitude is one of civic pride. The boosters have been proven right. The airport illustrates "the persistence of a vision," Joe Blake said.

Transportation Is Key

The story of DIA also illustrates the importance of transportation, as do the earliest records of the Denver Metro Chamber of Commerce. The chamber began as the Denver Board of Trade in 1867, "consolidating," as those early minutes put it, into the Denver Chamber of Commerce on January 15, 1884. Its objective was "to promote general prosperity in all the varied interests of Colorado and Denver." Even then the founders were thinking regionally.

The first resolution in the new chamber's minutes dealt with transportation. The Railroad Committee was directed "to confer with controlling authorities of railroads to readjust their pooled rates to recognize Denver as a commercial metropolis." The founders were thinking big. Territorial governor John Evans, a member of the board, resolved that Galveston, Texas, 840 miles away, should be designated "the future port of entry for the Rocky Mountain region." The chamber petitioned Congress to appropriate funds for Galveston harbor improvements. It also moved, in the blunt words of the minutes of that first meeting, "to shake down Congress for lots 28 and 29 in block 46, on Larimer Street, east Denver, for Commerce building."

The chamber's official birth came roughly fifteen years after the city faced its first major challenge. The story has been told so often it has become a cliché, but that doesn't make it any less relevant. Denver always has fretted about being left out, left behind; for a time, it appeared that the new city would find itself in just that unfortunate position. In the nineteenth century, when railroads were expanding westward, they either went south of Denver, through Albuquerque, New Mexico, or north, through Cheyenne, Wyoming. The 14,000-foot peaks west of Denver were too much of an obstacle. Shortly after the Civil War, when Union Pacific decided to route its transcontinental trains through Cheyenne, the Denver Board of Trade decided to move, and move fast. It raised $300,000 in a week's time to build a railroad spur line to Cheyenne. That was an astounding amount of money for the time, comparable to more than $5 million in the economy of 2009. On June 22, 1870, eleven months after the last spike in the intercontinental railroad was driven into a wooden tie at Promontory Summit, Utah, a Denver and Pacific Railway train chugged into Denver.

An 1870s engraving of the Denver Station of the Kansas Pacific, Denver Pacific, and Colorado Central Railroads. Photo courtesy of the Denver Public Library Western History Collection, Z-169.

The arrival of the railroad assured that Denver would continue to grow. "We thought we were doing the same with the airport," said Bob Albin, whose involvement with airport planning stretches back three decades. ("It really ought to be named Albin International Airport," one admirer said.) The airport "undoubtedly would never have been successful without business involvement," Albin said. And, he added, DIA wouldn't have happened without Peña, a "tremendous visionary and very good administrator" who was "tough as nails" in dealing with airport problems and airport opposition.

Peña served two terms, and it was left to his successor as mayor, Wellington Webb, to deal with the nuts and bolts—and the politics—of actually bringing the dream to reality. The record shows it was not easy. Things were much more complicated than they were in the time of the railroad barons a century earlier. "Gone are the days when leaders would come together and it would happen," said James "Skip" Spensley, the attorney whose diplomatic approach to problem solving cleared many of the obstacles to building DIA.

One of the differences is Coloradans' insistence on having a say in public investments. Fewer than half the states have a formalized process by which ordinary citizens can circulate petitions to put issues to a popular vote. Colorado is one of them, and Coloradans have taken ample advantage of that opportunity. Sometimes it creates problems. Most Colorado officeholders are term-limited, which eliminates a good deal of the incentive for entering into long-range planning. Thanks to another citizen initiative, Denver had to get Adams County's approval to expand its boundaries to include the new airport site. The Colorado state legislature is the only one of the fifty that cannot raise any tax without approval of a majority of voters.

That last restriction, the so-called TABOR amendment, has made it more difficult to invest in public infrastructure. But it also forces those who see a legitimate role for government, and a need for the things that government invests in, to work together for the common good. Business leaders were heavily involved in the bipartisan campaign to relax those restrictions for five years so the state budget could recover from a decade of artificially slowed growth.

Business also was involved in the ballot-issue campaigns that produced the Scientific and Cultural Facilities District, a fractional sales-tax addition that provides supplemental funding for museums, theatres, orchestras, and the Denver Zoo. Citizens don't always approve everything they're presented—they turned down funding for the 1976 Olympics and several mass-transit projects before finally approving what is perhaps the nation's most ambitious light-rail system. But when voters were convinced there was a need, they were enthusiastic supporters—of new sports venues, a rebuilt convention center, highway improvements, bonds for schools and libraries. Private developers, feeding off this enthusiasm, built new retail centers and downtown residential developments.

"An astounding public psyche" emerged from that list of late-twentieth-century accomplishments, Tom Clark said, "a sense that we can do this." It pulled Denver out of its economic doldrums. As one prominent example, "We could never have built the airport without the recession," Clark said.

"There's far more cooperation today than there was twenty years ago," former mayor Peña said. Of the level of regional cooperation in the Denver metropolitan area, he said, "I am willing to bet...[it] is far better than 95 percent of metro areas around the country."

And it has been noticed. Clark was impressed that former British prime minister Tony Blair sent a team of fourteen people "to just two places in America to find out how do you do regional economies—and it was Atlanta and us."

"When I first ran for mayor," Peña said, "the reputation of the Denver metro area was that we could not get anything done." Now that has changed. Metro communities have found a way to work together in luring new business instead of engaging in competing concession offers. "We decided to find a way to work together in attracting companies...I think we have learned in the metro community that we're all in this together...And the business community and chamber played a big part in that."

The regional partnering "paid off in real stuff, in real jobs," Clark said. In the search for new businesses, "We're closing 62 percent of our deals, and our closest competitors do 32 percent."

"We've been giving this regional message for thirty-five years," Clark added. "The other thing is the nature of this physical space, this sense of aspiration. This still is the West, and we're not afraid to innovate. We have to look outward, because we're a tiny little pod of affluence in the middle of a giant empty space."

Denver, 1860–1864

View of the *Rocky Mountain News* and surrounding buildings in Denver. William N. Byers founded the *Rocky Mountain News*, putting out the first issue on April 23, 1859. Photo courtesy of the Denver Public Library Western History Collection, Z-1520.

Chapter 2
Leadership

Compared with some other places, Colorado has a shortage of major corporate headquarters and old money. And it seems to have suffered a particularly rough period in the latter part of the first decade of the twenty-first century, when some corporate giants such as Qwest, Frontier Airlines, Coors Brewing Company, and First Data moved their headquarters—and their major decision makers—elsewhere.

Under most circumstances, the lack of a high-powered establishment with old money and leadership authority could be a major disadvantage to getting things done in a community. Yet, somehow, the state has managed to turn the lack of a traditional hierarchy into an advantage. Colorado, and its booming capital city, Denver, aren't governed by an elite. A newcomer doesn't have to buy a seat at the table. There are opportunities for the willing—and the energetic—to have an early and significant impact upon arrival.

Chamber staff tell a story about a businessman who had recently moved to Denver from Southern California. He wanted to know "what it takes" to get involved in the Denver cultural scene. Clark told him, well, it's mostly a matter of volunteering, commitment, a willingness to participate, that sort of thing. No, said the newcomer; that's not what I mean. I mean, *how much* does it take? In Huntington Beach, where he had come from, it took at least a quarter million dollars, he said.

John Welles, then executive director of the Denver Museum of Natural History (now the Denver Museum of Nature and Science) described Denver's civic leadership situation to the *New York Times* in a June 12, 1991, interview. It's an accurate summation of what many believe, and justifiably so. "The leadership of Denver tends to be diffuse, fragmented," Welles told the *Times*. "In Dallas or Minneapolis, if you want to get something done, you can get twenty or thirty people together for a meeting and make things happen. We can't do that. And I think perhaps that's because we're not a headquarters town."

There is also a constant supply of newcomers. "Denver and Colorado became a place where everybody was from someplace else," said John Frew, who ran the ballot-issue campaigns in 1988 and 1989 that cleared the way for Denver to build its new airport. Not surprisingly, Frew was from someplace else, too. He came to Colorado from Iowa in 1985 to run the campaign of former US senator Timothy Wirth.

Denver is comparatively young by world standards, barely 150 years old. It began as a raw and isolated frontier outpost, a place where two rather modest watercourses met, where fur trappers came to trade and Native Americans came to camp among the shimmering cottonwoods. The first settlement of Europeans dates to 1815, when two French trading posts went into business at the confluence of the South Platte River and Cherry Creek. In 1851, the fledgling federal government signed the Fort Laramie treaty, ceding the land from the Platte River to the Arkansas River to the Arapaho and Cheyenne tribes.

The discovery of gold changed everything.

History tends to be written from a political perspective. But most places, and their governments, are created by people looking for a better way of life—and, not coincidentally, a way to make a living. That means buying and selling,

William Larimer led a Georgia party of gold-seekers who found the first significant gold deposit in the Rocky Mountain region along the South Platte River. Photo courtesy of the Denver Public Library Western History Collection, F-25398.

and business. Denver was a product of the nineteenth-century gold rush that came a decade after gold was discovered in California. A prospecting party from Auraria, Georgia, found the first significant gold deposit in the Rocky Mountain region along the South Platte River, south of the river's confluence with Cherry Creek, in the summer of 1858. Word spread quickly. A party led by William H. Larimer, a land speculator from Leavenworth, in Kansas Territory, was among the seekers. On November 22 of that year Larimer and his partners founded the Denver City Town Company. They named the ramshackle settlement for James W. Denver, governor of Kansas Territory.

Over the next two years, from 1859 to 1860, some one hundred thousand fortune-seekers migrated to the new boomtown. They didn't have an easy time of it. John P. Horton, part of a group of prospectors from Chicago, wrote this plaintive letter to his wife on May 18, 1859:

> Well, we were not here more than three or four days before we saw that the reports had been greatly exaggerated in regard to the extent of the richness of the mines...On our arrival we found a great many disheartened, and preparing to leave for the States, and indeed we met many such on the way who urged us to desist, turn and go home. A great many did so, but you know when I start for a place I go through, if I live to do it.

The "Pikes Peak or Bust" gold rush, which obviously from its name included more than just Denver, prompted the federal government to establish the Colorado Territory in early 1861. Denver City, the municipality succeeding the founding corporation, was formally incorporated in November of that year.

There was a bit of a settlement problem, though, and it wasn't handled in a particularly humanitarian fashion. Territorial governor John Evans and William N. Byers, publisher of the city's first newspaper, the *Rocky Mountain News*, led a movement to remove the Cheyenne and Arapaho tribes from land that Denver's ambitious founders coveted. The original Fort Laramie Treaty with the native tribes was replaced with the Fort Wise Treaty, establishing the Sand Creek Reservation. Many tribe leaders refused to sign it. Indian agent William Bent, after whom Bent's Fort is named, resigned his position in protest.

By today's standards, what Evans and Byers did to displace the Indians would certainly be considered questionable at best. Yet they were also the ones who laid the foundations for the new city's inevitable growth. On November 13, 1867, they founded the Denver Board of Trade, the business-boosting, growth-touting, visionary group that eventually became the Denver Metro Chamber of Commerce.

In quick succession during those early years, more gold deposits, and then silver, were discovered in the mountains, and Denver was flourishing. It had become the main supply center for the mountain mining camps, and it needed a railroad. The business community led the campaign, raising money and buttonholing the people who could make things happen, and in 1870, three railroads came to town, led by the Denver and Pacific Railway in June, and then followed by the Kansas Pacific and the Colorado Central. In the twenty years after the railroads arrived, Denver's population exploded from 4,760 to nearly 107,000, second only to San Francisco in the West.

Three Major Legacies

When former chamber president M. Doak Jacoway talks about the city's future, he likes to invoke three figures from the past. Three imports to the Mountain West, he said, made the Denver area what it is today. Their contributions were all in vital areas, all things that today's regional residents may take for granted, but that were innovations in their day and absolutely essential to the area's future. They deserve a little more explanation.

The three pioneers were Walter S. Cheesman, who was primarily responsible for establishing a stable water supply for the city; Mayor Robert W. Speer, who championed intelligent, attractive urban planning; and Mayor Benjamin F. Stapleton, who put the city at the forefront of commercial airline transportation. And all had traveled a long way to make their mark in the new city.

Cheesman, originally from New York, came to Denver somewhat late in the nineteenth century. Denver had been dipping its drinking water out of Cherry Creek and the Platte. It was comparatively clean, but that wouldn't do for a real city. There were water entrepreneurs before Cheesman. In 1870, the year the railroads came to town, Denver also got its first municipal water supplier. Through the rest of the nineteenth century, a series of water companies fought for the right to serve the growing city's needs. But finally, Cheesman's Denver City Water Company drove its last major competitor out of business

Walter Scott Cheesman and his water company were instrumental in providing water to the growing city of Denver. The Cheesman Dam and Reservoir, built in 1905, was named in his honor. Photo courtesy of the Denver Public Library Western History Collection, F-11658.

by offering water for free—the ultimate tactic in a price war. It, along with several other smaller companies serving other parts of the region, merged into the Denver Union Water Company in October 1894. The new company, from which today's Denver Water Department was formed, was headed by Cheesman and David Moffat, whose name is on the railroad-and-water tunnel that pierces the Continental Divide west of Denver. Another major achievement of those early years was construction of the Cheesman Dam and Reservoir on the South Platte River. Completed in 1905, it is still a major provider for Denver Water's more than 1 million customers. The region finally had a reliable supply of water—absolutely necessary to assure its continued success.

Robert W. Speer was elected mayor three times during the years between 1904 and 1918. As an advocate of the "City Beautiful" movement then in vogue, he inspired the untamed young city to remake itself, taking advantage of Denver's sunny climate and inspiring natural setting by employing proper urban planning and building parks, fountains, statues, and tree-lined boulevards. Civic Center, the mountain parks system, a natural history museum, and expansion of the city zoo were accomplished under his leadership, as was construction of Denver Civic Auditorium, site of the 1908 Democratic National Convention. Historian Tom Noel has called the Pennsylvania native, who came to Denver at age twenty-three, the city's most powerful mayor, an energetic tuberculosis survivor and real estate developer who "seemed to be everywhere." In a January 7, 1907, speech to the Denver City Council—Noel called it a "pep talk"—Speer shared

Robert W. Speer was an advocate of the City Beautiful movement and emphasized urban planning and building parks, fountains, statues, and tree-lined boulevards. Photo courtesy of the Denver Public Library Western History Collection, F-28604.

his vision: "We are in a plastic state. As the twig is bent so the tree will grow... Denver can be made one of the ordinary cities of the country, or she can be made the Paris of America. It will cost money, but this investment will pay ten dollars for every one spent."

Benjamin F. Stapleton embraced air travel before most people took it seriously. He was Denver's mayor for two eight-year stretches, from 1923 to 1931 and from 1935 to 1947. Born in Kentucky and educated in Ohio, Stapleton came to Denver after he was discharged from the US Army in 1889. He was responsible for a great many civic improvements, including a major expansion of the city's parks system and completion of the Civic Center. But the project for which he is most remembered, the one requiring his best skills of political perseverance, is the one that eventually was named for him, Stapleton International Airport. Yet Stapleton's reputation is tarnished by his ties to the Ku Klux Klan—ties that didn't fully come to light until after he had left office. The *Rocky Mountain News* reported in 2000 an excerpt from a speech Stapleton had given decades earlier: "I will work with the Klan and for the Klan in the coming election, heart and soul," Stapleton vowed at a

Berthoud Ski Area, owned by the City of Denver, was part of the mountain park system conceived of by Mayor Speer. Photo courtesy of the Denver Metro Chamber of Commerce.

Klan rally. "And if I am re-elected, I will give the Klan the kind of administration it wants."

Stapleton, as it turned out, may not have been as malleable as the Klan had hoped. And the Klan's hold on power in Colorado was comparatively brief, if nonetheless embarrassing. Stapleton may have been a somewhat flawed visionary, but his commitment to promoting air travel was a lasting legacy.

Even so, Stapleton's airport ignited controversy in the late 1920s that foreshadows what critics were saying about the new Denver International Airport seventy years later. Robert Stapp, Stapleton airport's public affairs manager from 1971 to 1982, said in his foreword to Jeff Miller's history of the now-closed airport that "when the Denver Municipal Airport was opened in October 1929, it was variously described as 'one of the most complete and safe aerial stations in the world'—and as a massive boondoggle." By today's standards, it was hardly an expensive investment. The 640 acres for this daring addition to the city had been acquired for just $143,000.

Benjamin F. Stapleton was an early supporter of air travel. Denver's Stapleton International Airport was eventually named for him. Photo courtesy of the Denver Public Library Western History Collection, F-11554.

Modern Denver simply wouldn't be where it is today if it hadn't aggressively pursued the latest transportation options, Jacoway said. It needs to be a hub. Its political and business leaders have recognized this over the years, and whatever flaws they might have had, the good ones have always had that vision in mind.

"Our business community is about as engaged as any business community in the United States," said Bruce Benson, a former oil industry executive and state Republican chairman who is now president of the University of Colorado system. Benson, a graduate of CU who returned to Colorado in 1975, is one of many examples of Coloradans who by choice found an opportunity to get involved and turned it ultimately to personal success and community benefit. "Until [former governor] Dick Lamm put me on the Colorado Commission of Higher Education, I hadn't done much… I had to make a conscious effort to go out and meet the business leadership," Benson said. Lamm was once considered a liberal Democrat; Benson is a strong Republican. But that's one of the strengths of the region's leadership. It is a bipartisan group, and it looks for solutions that aren't politically divisive.

Benson points out that Denver's leadership is always changing. People tend to get attached to the region, as he did, and once they get here, they stay. But there's always room for new movers and shakers. "We've lost some companies," he said, and the old corporate mainstays are moving in new directions. "Even Coors has a new flavor," Benson said. But even with all the change, there's a constant: elected officials, businesspeople, and educators all appreciate the need to get involved. "There's new blood. But the new entrepreneurs care about the community." Denver once had a reputation, Benson and others concede, of not being able to get things done. "By God, you can get 'em done now," he said.

Dick Fleming

When people speak of the business community's involvement in community projects, they always mention Richard C. D. Fleming. "Greater Dick" Fleming—flamboyant, eloquent, supremely confident, and competent—played a significant role in helping Federico Peña

Dick Fleming had been a private developer and a city planner in Atlanta before coming to Denver. Photo courtesy of the Denver Public Library Western History Collection.

establish himself as a regional force to be reckoned with. That observation comes from Peña's successor, Wellington Webb, who said that Fleming had a take-charge style that some thought was almost too aggressive. Fleming doesn't deny it; when he took charge, at about the time Peña was settling in to his second term, the chamber had become "too mellow; it wasn't the agent of change it is now," Fleming said.

Fleming was a sub-cabinet officer at the Department of Housing and Urban Development when he was recruited to come to Denver in 1980. Fleming had been a private developer and a city planner in Atlanta, involved in a number of major projects, including the expansion of Hartsfield International Airport. He began his fourteen-year transformational career in Denver as both the founding president and CEO of the Downtown Denver Partnership. Then, in 1987, Dick Schlosberg, publisher of *The Denver Post*, recruited him to take over a similar dual role at the Denver Metro Chamber and a new effort at promoting regionalism, the Greater Denver Corporation (GDC).

For a while, what is today the Denver Metro Chamber of Commerce was the Greater Denver Chamber of Commerce—a "somewhat controversial" name change that nonetheless sent an important signal throughout the region, Fleming believes. Tom Clark, who had been hired away from the Fort Collins Chamber of Commerce to be the chamber's economic development director, eventually became president of the GDC.

The Greater Denver Corporation coincides with Fleming's leadership of the chamber. From 1987 to 1995, the GDC raised $14 million to create new jobs and an economic recovery. It backed projects such as a new convention center, a new baseball-only stadium—and, of course, a new airport—that were responsible for creating a total of 400,000 jobs in the metropolitan area. Dolores Wilson, the last president of the GDC, wrote this in her introduction to Bill Hornby's "Eye on the Horizon," a history of the eight-year GDC effort:

> The Greater Denver Corporation has always had its "eye on the horizon." It has been a catalyst in many major projects such as the convention center and airport which will serve future generations. At the same time, it dealt with more immediate problems including the creation of high-quality jobs. But even then, the GDC chose to be innovative. It established and funded a new way for the metropolitan area to work together to attract new companies and

assist existing ones to grow. The legacy of the Greater Denver Corporation is the Metro Denver Network; the cooperative philosophy of the MDN will serve this community well in the future.

Fleming was recruited by St. Louis in 1994, and, he concedes, the fact that the Missouri city is home to twenty-one Fortune 1000 companies' headquarters was a factor in his decision to relocate. But that kind of establishment tradition has its good and bad points, he said. "It's one of the challenges a city like St. Louis has; 70 percent of the people who live here have always lived here."

The same is definitely not true of Denver. When Fleming came to Denver in 1980, some five thousand people a month were on the move—some out of the city; many more into it. "Denver has so many newcomers," Fleming said. "That creates extraordinary energy and also poses a different kind of challenge." The metro area, and all of Colorado's growing areas, produce entrepreneurs who become civic leaders; people like cable TV pioneer Bill Daniels, oilman Sam Gary, and former University of Denver chancellor Daniel Ritchie.

This mobile, sometimes restless community has shown an ability to rally when times are tough. Roy Romer, another energetic leader, was elected governor the same week Fleming was hired to head the chamber. This was in the mid-1980s, when the economy was in one of the worst of its periodic weak spells. Fleming saved an issue of *Forbes* magazine from that period that had a piece about Denver headlined "Rocky Mountain Low." Essentially, he said, the *Forbes* article concluded that "you can't fall off the floor." He also saved, in the same display box, a *Time* magazine story from ten years later headlined "Rocky Mountain High."

There was "a remarkable civic energy that came forward" during those down days, Fleming recalled. "The overriding message was: We have a crisis, the business community needs to step up and deal with the political community. But they don't want to do it unless the region stops squabbling and starts cooperating."

Fleming, when he headed the Denver Metro Chamber, was "a bigger-than-life CEO," said Clark, who has held a number of top chamber positions over the years, including head of the Greater Denver Corporation. When Fleming took over, "there wasn't a lot of regional thinking in those days." Now that mindset has changed. Regional governments worked together to win voter approval of infrastructure improvements. They meet regularly to talk about their mutual goals. They stepped up to offer solutions when the light-rail system, FasTracks, was hurt by the global recession and saw a serious decline of the sales tax revenue it needed to complete a major expansion. The region, Clark said, has "developed a custom" of working together. Former Aurora mayor Paul Tauer, one of the leaders of the Metro Mayors Caucus, has been known to refer to the airport as "our metro regional project."

That regional approach is also reflected in two programs the Denver Metro Chamber Leadership Foundation has established to promote the continuing development of civic leaders, to introduce those who are new to the community into how things work here, and to open the doors to enhanced civic involvement for developing and active leaders alike.

Impact Denver is an introductory civic leadership program, as the application form explains it, "specifically designed for Metro Denver's next generation of community leaders." It's aimed at professionals who are just getting started in the Denver area and who want to learn more about the region and its opportunities for civic involvement. In a half-dozen sessions over a six-month period, including an all-day class retreat, participants hear from community leaders and experts about the region's economy, its key industries, its political and social issues, and its philanthropic and service traditions.

Leadership Denver is for those who already have established themselves as community leaders or have shown strong potential for getting to that point: "senior policy-shaping responsibilities and positions of leadership, both as a professional and as a civic volunteer." It's one of the oldest community leadership programs in the country. It began in 1974 and, like Impact Denver, serves a valuable networking role, said Maureen McDonald, executive director of the Denver Metro Chamber Leadership Foundation. It's an extensive, eleven-month program usually involving around fifty-five leaders representative of the community's diversity. The classes develop a long-term service project to implement in the year following their class participation. While Impact Denver is for those just beginning their civic commitments, Leadership Denver is for those who want to expand and enhance their involvement.

A 2010 study by Battelle's Technology Partnership Practice selected the leadership foundation's programs as among six "best in class" offerings around the country. The selection was based, McDonald said, on the level of engagement of the programs' alumni, the involvement of youth in their communities, financing strategies, links to regional priorities, the way the programs evaluate their own effectiveness, and their willingness to share ideas.

"Business and local government officials have developed a very strong working relationship within the region," a consulting and policy development firm called FutureWorks wrote in its assessment of the Denver region and the various structures that make regional cooperation easier and more effective. The assessment further outlined the web of relationships:

> The mayors of the 31 municipalities formed the Metro Mayors Caucus in 1993 to work collaboratively on regional issues ranging from growth management to workforce housing and transportation. In 1999, business, local government, and citizen group leaders formed the Transit Alliance, which is housed at the Denver Metro Chamber, supported by the Metro Mayors Caucus and staffed by two environmental leaders. The Metro Mayors Caucus meetings are hosted by the Denver Metro Chamber, which formed a Local Affairs Committee in 2004 to focus on supporting collaborative initiatives with local governments.

FutureWorks also noted that in 2002, "with another economic crisis underway, economic development officials and business leaders criticized the Chamber for letting the Metro Denver Network falter." The chamber responded in 2003 by bringing back one of its chief critics, Tom Clark, who had previously been the chamber's executive vice president but left in 1998 to run the Jefferson Economic Council. The chamber created the Metro Denver EDC and made Clark executive vice president of economic development.

The embrace of regionalism has grown considerably since Leadership Denver began more than thirty-five years ago, and the spirit of "we're all in this together" has helped the metropolitan area weather the fickle winds of the changing economy. Business and political leaders agree that the new airport couldn't have been built if it hadn't been for the economic downturn of the late 1980s. The economic crisis essentially forced competitive municipal entities to cooperate, said John Frew, whose political savvy is given a great deal of the credit for the success of the two campaigns that won a healthy voter endorsement of the new airport.

In some ways, Frew said, the Denver area would have had an easier time of it if Colorado US senator Gary Hart had been elected president in 1984 or 1988. Former Georgia governor Jimmy Carter, elected president in 1976, "made Atlanta what it is," Frew said. Old money helped Atlanta, too—something that Denver has only in short supply. But you don't need old money or an entrenched power structure to succeed in the Denver area. And, Frew said, "You don't have to hit home runs; you can bunt your way around the bases."

Performance counts for more than pedigree. Former Denver mayor Wellington Webb said that has always been the test for success in these parts: "If you can get that wagon train across the Rockies, you're hired. If you can't get that wagon train across the Rockies, you're fired."

In the Denver area, Webb said, "There are so many opportunities for people to get involved...different organizations where they can make a difference, and they're accepted. And they're accepted on performance...This is a city of organizations and joiners, and you can find your niche, you can find your place anywhere."

Denver, 1865

View of Fifteenth Street. Photo courtesy of the Denver Public Library Western History Collection, X-23653.

Chapter 3
Colorado's Political Environment

Coloradans like to think they have comparatively clean government. In truth, there has been relatively little corruption in Colorado politics over the years. And yet, because the state constitution makes it very easy to put an issue on the ballot, Colorado voters have enacted some restrictions that seem to be punishing their local public servants for the well-publicized misdeeds of politicos elsewhere.

Basically conservative politically, Colorado voters have enacted some pioneering as well as some problematic innovations over the years, both liberal and conservative in nature. The people Coloradans elect to office, for the most part, seem to behave more honorably than politicians elsewhere. Or it may be only that the requirements voters have imposed on their political leaders prevent them from doing much mischief—or much of anything else, for that matter.

Colorado is part of the politically unpredictable West. Mostly that means the Intermountain West. The coastal states have been fairly reliably liberal for years. But Colorado has a mixed history. It's fair to say it has been politically conservative through most of its years as a state. But it's a fiscal conservatism, not a social one. During the 1990s, the state was consistently Republican. But that changed starting with the first elections of the twenty-first century. Now it's more like what it was thirty years earlier—politically balanced, possibly a bit more liberal than before.

In the terminology of twenty-first-century political punditry, Colorado has been considered a "red" state. Because of its history, it is typically expected to favor Republican candidates over Democrats, conservative policies over liberal ones, and small government over government-driven stimulus programs. But recent elections show this is not necessarily true. Colorado voters, even those in predictably partisan places like Denver (Democratic) or Colorado Springs (Republican), have an independent streak.

One indicator of Colorado's basic conservatism, voter registration, shows that Republicans have had an almost constant plurality through the decades. But it is no more than a plurality. Unaffiliated voters, notoriously unpredictable but famously flexible, make up a full third of Colorado's electorate. That trend toward disaffiliation has been much remarked about in national politics recently, but it has been a fact of life in Colorado for decades. Democrats usually are in third place in registration numbers, but that doesn't mean they don't do well at the polls. Toward the

Former president Theodore Roosevelt (in carriage) waves to Denver spectators on August 29, 1910. Photo courtesy of the Denver Public Library Western History Collection, Harry M. Rhoads, Rh-655.

end of the first decade of the twenty-first century, Colorado Democrats controlled a solid majority of the congressional delegation, both chambers of the legislature, and the governor's office. But for most of the preceding four decades, the same was true of the Republican Party. Going into the 2004 elections, the governor's office and both houses of the state legislature were in the hands of the Republicans; both US senators were Republicans, and the state's congressional district seats were divided 5 to 2 in favor of the Republican Party. After the 2008 elections, the governor's office and the legislative chambers were controlled by the Democrats, and the congressional ratio was 5 to 2 in the Democrats' favor. It had been forty years since Democrats had held that much power in Colorado.

Well into 2010, Colorado voter registration numbers were all within a percentage point of 33 percent for Democrats, Republicans, and unaffiliated voters, as reported by the secretary of state's elections division. It doesn't get any closer than that. When a Republican tide swept through the nation in the 2010 midterm elections, it seemed to leave Colorado high and dry. Republicans did pick up two seats in Congress, and a narrow margin in the state House of Representatives, but Democrats John Hickenlooper (governor) and Michael Bennet (US Senate) also won. And voters handily rejected some radically antigovernment ballot issues.

Denver, the state capital, has a tradition of Democratic politics. Democrats outnumber Republicans in the city and county of Denver by more than 2 to 1, even though there may be one or two Republicans on the city council at any given time, and an equally small number of Republicans representing the city in the state legislature. Through much of its history, Denver has been represented in Congress by a Democrat—Democratic women, in fact, since the early 1970s. Patricia Schroeder served twenty-four years, retiring in 1996 to be succeeded by Diana DeGette. Boulder and Adams counties, to the north of the city, and Pueblo County, at the south end of the Front Range, also are dominated by Democratic Party politics.

But for the most part, it's not the old-style Democratic machine politics of big labor, big spending, and big taxes. Colorado Democrats, no matter where they live, have to be centrists if they're going to succeed. They have to know how to get along with the business community. They join, and even create, chambers of commerce. And yet, after several years of controlling both chambers of the legislature and the governor's office, they lately have been following the Republicans' example of what happens after a political party gets used to power. Its activists and fringes get more assertive, and the centrists have to battle their own party to keep from veering off from the middle of the road into a ditch.

Republicans, after so many years in control at the state and local level, have drifted into two camps: the fiscal conservatives and the social conservatives. The fiscal-only conservatives tend to be more moderate in their overall outlook, more willing to work with middle-of-the-road Democrats to actually get things done. Several of them, in fact—including former governor Bill Owens—joined forces with the Denver Metro Chamber of Commerce and a majority of Democrats to pass a ballot initiative in 2005 that put a temporary hold on a spending limitation that had severely restricted the state's budgeting options. The social-agenda Republicans, who also tend to be more adamant in their opposition to government spending, were among the strongest opponents of the moratorium, which in the end passed with only a 52 percent favorable vote in an off-year election that had only a 40 percent turnout.

Republicans are the dominant party in more than two-thirds of the state's sixty-four counties. Republican voter registration is at least 2 to 1 over Democrats in El Paso County, the home of Colorado Springs. The same lopsided ratio also holds in Mesa County on the Western Slope and in the Fifth Congressional District south of Denver. The Sixth District, composed mostly of the well-to-do southern Denver suburbs, has voted Republican since it was created in 1982.

Colorado's reputation for solid Republicanism, at least until recently, is largely a result of its population growth during the 1990s. The total state population increased by roughly a third during that decade, with much of the influx coming from middle-to-upper-class families migrating from the more conservative areas of California and, to a lesser extent, Texas, looking for better jobs and lower taxes.

Where People Want to Be

Colorado is one of the fastest growing states in the country. And Denver in just the past few years has become one of the state's fastest-growing counties. After years of declining population, Denver began to grow again as new residential areas were developed and the number of cultural, dining, and entertainment opportunities in the downtown area

Denver's Sixteenth Street Mall, one of the many attractions of the city. Photo © 2011 Eric Lars Bakke.

increased. A 2009 survey by the Pew Foundation found that when all factors were considered together, Denver was the city where most people would rather live if they were to move from where they lived now. In a release headlined "Denver Tops List of Favorite Cities," the Pew Research Center's Social & Demographic Trends project found that "nearly half (46%) of the public would rather live in a different type of community from the one they're living in now." Where, exactly? Denver was named by 43 percent, followed by San Diego at 40 percent, and Seattle at 38 percent.

The US Census Bureau in the spring of 2010 estimated that the population of the city itself had exceeded 600,000, with the rest of the metro area accounting for another 2 million or more. The new estimates make the city, with its coterminous county boundaries, the fastest-growing county in the state, and one of the fastest-growing in the county.

Colorado attracts people. It builds on its reputation of having a healthy, active, well-educated population. One-third of its residents have at least a bachelor's degree, compared to 24 percent for the United States as a whole. Its median household income is 10 percent higher than the national average. It's not an especially diverse population ethnically, although like much of the Southwest it has a high proportion of residents of Latino heritage. Of Colorado's more than 5 million residents, 20 percent are of Hispanic origin and slightly more than 4 percent are African American, according to the US Census Bureau. Most of the black population is concentrated in the Denver area. Racial problems are minimal, although the legislature often finds itself debating what to do about illegal immigration from Mexico.

Thirty years ago, when other cities were having serious problems with racial strife, the Denver area escaped much of the turmoil. And yet there is a history of racial politics in Denver. For a comparatively brief period during the 1920s—and despite the city's minuscule black population—the Ku Klux Klan exerted tremendous influence over city and state politics. During those years, Colorado had 55,000 members of the Ku Klux Klan, roughly 5 percent of the state's population. The Klan ran Denver city government. Clarence Morley, an obscure Denver District Court judge and high-ranking Klan officer, was elected governor. Rice Means—a Klan member who had been appointed Denver's city attorney—won a short-term US Senate seat. Benjamin F. Stapleton, who didn't widely advertise his Klan membership, was elected Denver's mayor with support from both Klan and anti-Klan forces. The political mastermind behind the Klan's brief grip on the reins of government power was a portly physician named John Galen Locke. According to the Colorado State Archives, "Locke focused less on the overt violence and racism that characterized many other Klan groups and more on creating one of the strongest political machines that Colorado had thus far seen." As *The Denver Post* wrote, "Beyond any doubt the KKK is the largest and most cohesive, most efficiently organized political force in the state." Klan candidates won the 1924 statewide elections in a landslide.

In fairness, it should be pointed out that Stapleton was a better candidate than the field running against him for mayor, some of whom were accused of corruption. And his embrace of Klan idealogy was not as reliable as Locke may have wanted. Locke launched a recall campaign against him, forcing him to run again—and with that ploy, some say, increasing his influence over the mayor after whom Denver's first airport was named. Stapleton may have been a visionary about the importance of commercial air travel, but his early political career, at least, has a dark side to it. Ironically, the new neighborhood named after his airport, and built over its abandoned runways, is one of the country's most successful manifestations of "new urbanism," a diverse, compact, integrated area of middle-class families and singles.

As further evidence of their rejection of racial politics, Denver voters beginning in the 1980s elected a Hispanic, Federico Peña, to two terms as mayor, and an African American, Wellington Webb, to three terms as head of city government. At the state level, Colorado in 2009 had the only state legislature with African Americans in its highest-ranking leadership posts, House Speaker Terrance Carroll and Senate President Peter Groff.

Some thirty years after its flirtation with the Klan, the city government of Denver found itself embarrassed by another shameful episode. During the 1950s, dozens of Denver police were involved in burglaries and pettier crimes like payoffs and stealing money from corpses and accident victims. The corruption spread to suburban counties, too, with law enforcement officers charged with crimes ranging from breaking and entering to embezzlement. More than two hundred safes were cracked open by cops, with a total take of $250,000, which would be almost $2 million in today's dollars. "By the time of their exposure," *Time* magazine reported on November 3, 1961, "there were at least five organized teams of expert safecrackers on the force."

Despite some anomalies such as the Klan years and the Denver police scandal, Colorado politics and politicians are comparatively clean. Even before Colorado voters made open government meetings and open government records a constitutional requirement, there was a tradition of transparency. Colorado politics are admirably above-board. Much to the frustration of generations of reformers and muckrakers, there is not an ingrained tradition of graft and corruption all too prevalent in some other, older states. "Pay-for-play" is not part of the political psyche. Colorado's attorney general, John Suthers, has said that when he was US attorney for the state, he had a difficult time finding evidence of the sort of malfeasance federal justice authorities assumed had to be happening everywhere.

One might think that a comparatively clean and competent government would foster a contented and cooperative form of civic engagement, with citizens trusting their elected officials to mostly do the right thing. That hasn't been the case. Colorado's politicians have been painted with a broad brush, in many cases suffering for the bad reputations of their counterparts in other states and in Congress.

Initiative and Innovation

Many of Colorado's innovations in governance helped convince *Megatrends* author John Naisbitt to name it one of ten "bellwether" states in his widely cited book, first published in 1982. Much of what Naisbitt cited in his economic analysis were private-sector innovations, but a significant component was what Coloradans had done to ensure better government. Many, if not most, of those trend-setting experiments were the result of citizen initiatives, questions placed on the statewide ballot by petition. Those ideas have evolved over the years from mostly liberal to mostly conservative in philosophy. On the liberal side, Colorado was one of the first states to adopt a nonpartisan selection process for judges, in 1966. Its "sunshine law" requirements for open government meetings, records, and financial reports date back to the 1972 election. On a more philosophically conservative note, it imposed term limits for elected officials in 1990 and a strict limit on government revenue in 1992.

Colorado adopted the initiative and referendum process in 1912 and is one of only twenty-four states that allow their citizens to change the laws that govern them by petitioning to put questions on a statewide ballot. It is one of only fifteen that permit this kind of citizen access to both the statutes and the state constitution. And, with a rather modest signature requirement that is the same for either statutory or constitutional amendments, it is arguably the easiest place in the country to put an issue on the ballot.

It is not an exaggeration to say that Colorado citizens have much more power than their state legislature has. In fact, Colorado citizens have rather consistently and earnestly been removing powers from their elected representatives.

Representative government in Colorado is frustrated by those two factors: Citizens who want to change the constitution face fewer obstacles, and as a result the legislature has fewer powers, than in any other state. Colorado has the only legislature in the country that can't raise tax rates without voter approval. Its elected officials have to try to juggle citizen-initiated constitutional amendments that both limit state government's spending increases to the rate of inflation and require it to increase spending—for public education—by more than the rate of inflation. Activists behind these changes say they are intended to correct an inefficient, overly partisan political process. But the "corrections" more often than not make the process less efficient and more political.

The ease of ballot access is difficult for some citizen activists to resist. In the 2008 election, for example, there were fourteen citizen-initiated changes on Colorado's statewide ballot, more than in any other state. Some of these proposals create problems for efficient governance, and some are even direct threats to the business community. From time to time, this drives the business community to come together again, either to oppose or support ballot issues.

Bipartisan Efforts

In 2005, a coalition of mostly Democratic state legislators, the Republican governor, and a bipartisan group of business leaders joined forces to push for passage of two legislative referendums designed to relieve the state from the strictures of a citizen initiative passed in 1992. The so-called TABOR amendment (a somewhat labored acronym for Taxpayer Bill of Rights) says that no tax increase can be passed without the approval of a majority of affected voters, and it also limits annual government revenue increases to no more than the rate of inflation,

The Daniels and Fisher Tower was the third tallest building in the United States when erected in 1910. The Kortz clock was built as an advertisement for Kortz Jewelers, (started business in Denver in 1893). Photo © 2011 Eric Lars Bakke.

adjusted for population growth. Its net effect has been to steadily reduce the state's ability to keep up with citizen demands for services. Combined with another citizen initiative that requires inflation-plus-1-percent increases in spending for public schools, kindergarten through high school, the result has been that other government services have to bear the brunt of reduced revenue. Higher education in particular has felt the impact of the government's inability to spend all the tax money it collected.

Referendums C and D were put before voters by the legislature. Referendum D was bonding authority for several proposed spending projects, but it failed. More than three hundred businesses and business groups, including the Denver Metro Chamber of Commerce and nine other chambers of commerce around the state, supported the Referendum C moratorium. It put a five-year hold on TABOR's requirement that the state had to return, in the form of tax refunds, any revenue that exceeded the 1992 amendment's inflation-based limit on annual increases. In good years, when Coloradans were spending more and earning more—and thus paying more in sales and income taxes—the state had to give extra money back. Referendum C passed in an off-year election in 2005, with only a 40 percent voter turnout and a favorable vote of just 52 percent.

"Referendum C's passage was a statement by the electorate that assured business that Colorado's transportation network and higher education system would be able to meet their needs," said Joe Blake, then president and CEO of the Denver Metro Chamber of Commerce. "We saw a spike of activity of out-of-state businesses interested in relocating here when Referendum C passed." But the campaign also created some resentment, especially in the fiscally conservative Republican Party. Bruce Benson, the former GOP state chairman, supported the original TABOR amendment in 1992—but also the moratorium in 2005. "We took care of the glitches [but] I still have people that won't talk with me over this thing," Benson said.

Business interests came together again after four initiatives, widely criticized as extreme and antibusiness, appeared headed for the ballot. The initiatives were a reaction to a "right to work" proposal to ban compulsory union membership, but were dropped by their mostly union supporters after a group including the Denver Metro Chamber came out against all five competing ballot issues. But "right to work" split business interests, with some chambers of commerce and business associations supporting it. In the end, the RTW initiative lost by 12 percentage points, 44 percent in favor to 56 percent against. So did almost everything else petitioned onto the crowded ballot in 2008.

An even broader coalition came together in 2010 to fight three ballot initiatives that would have further restricted government's ability to manage its finances. The two constitutional amendments and one statutory change would have cut a number of taxes, denied the state any ability to bond for long-term projects, and invalidated previous elections in which citizens had removed revenue restrictions on their local governments. Republicans, Democrats, unions, businesses, and just about anybody with anything to say about it went to work. They outspent a rather shadowy, largely anonymous group of proponents by about 200 to 1, and none of the measures got more than a quarter to a third of the vote. That could perhaps be seen as a gauge of the level of sympathy in the state for the "Tea Party" brand of antigovernment activism.

The Denver Metro Chamber also has backed attempts to reform the initiative process, but that's perhaps a more risky undertaking. The chamber's polling shows that almost a two-thirds majority of the public favors the existing easy ballot access. That same poll shows almost the opposite sentiment in the business community: a slightly larger proportion of business leaders, a bit more than two-thirds, would like to make it more difficult to change laws, and especially to amend the constitution, by popular referendum.

The 2008 election offered more evidence that the public may not be ready for change. A citizen initiative backed by House Speaker Andrew Romanoff, an effort to reconcile the conflicts between contradictory fiscal amendments in the constitution, lost by 8 percentage points. And a separate legislative referendum to make it more difficult to amend the constitution, and easier to amend state statutes, lost by 5 percentage points.

Denver, 1886–1901

A rooftop view northwest up Seventeenth Street in downtown Denver. Photo courtesy of the Denver Fublic Library Western History Collection, Rose & Hopkins, H-583.

Chapter 4
Businesses Come and Grow

In April 2010, a once-small telephone company based in a still-small Louisiana town took over one of Denver's corporate giants. The purchase of Qwest by CenturyTel, a telecommunications company based in Monroe, Louisiana, was another in a string of frustrating farewells to long-standing local icons.

How embarrassing. A city half the size of Pueblo, Colorado, three hundred miles from New Orleans, snaps up one of Colorado's few remaining Fortune 500 companies. But it wasn't the only blow to the region's civic pride. In 2009, First Data, an economic development plum when it arrived in 2001, moved back to Atlanta. Denver's resuscitated and popular favorite Frontier Airlines was acquired by Republic Airways and its headquarters moved to Indianapolis. And the corporate headquarters of MillerCoors, a brewer that still touts the Rocky Mountains in its advertising, moved to Chicago.

Had the region somehow become unattractive? Or was it, as several economic development experts figured, just a patch of bad luck?

Chalk it up to circumstance. The region still has an educated workforce, good schools, transportation, culture,

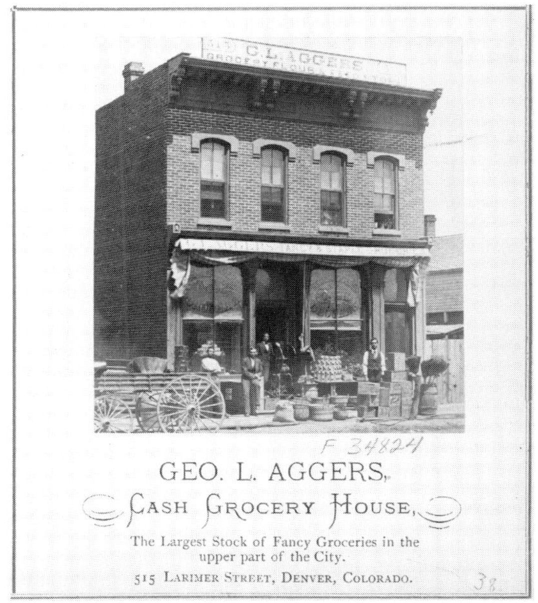

George L. Aggers was the largest stock of fancy groceries in the upper part of the city between 1869 and 1879. Photo courtesy of the Denver Public Library Western History Collection, Duhem Brothers, X-18510.

View of the Gates Rubber Company water tower, which stood from 1930 to 1950. The company was started in 1911 when Charles Gates Sr. bought the Colorado Tire and Leather Company in Denver. The company became an international corporation, selling garden hoses and fan belts, among many other products. Photo courtesy of the Denver Public Library Western History Collection, WHC Gates Corp., X-24532.

fine restaurants, low taxes, and an enviable lifestyle. "The quality of life is hard to beat," Doug Allen, director of global programs at the University of Denver Daniels School of Business told *The Denver Post* in a Qwest postmortem.

Perception isn't necessarily reality, either. In fact, by mid-2010, Colorado had had a seasonally adjusted net gain of 52,000 jobs since late 2003, when the Metro Denver EDC was created. Those employment figures came from the US Bureau of Labor Statistics, whose data also showed that over that same period Georgia lost 37,000 jobs and Indiana lost 96,000. In July 2010 alone, noted chamber president and CEO Kelly J. Brough, the Metro Denver EDC and all of its partners helped add 12,800 jobs to the region. Colorado also saw forty-five company headquarters move to the state over that same 2003 to 2010 period, Brough said.

They obviously aren't all Fortune 500 companies. The painful truth is that Colorado has seen a net decline from twelve Fortune 500 firms in 2007 to eight in 2010. It might have fallen to seven, except that DaVita, a major medical company in the business of providing kidney care, moved its headquarters to downtown Denver.

Through all the coming and going, though, small business also has remained a bright spot. And small business, as its advocates like to point out whenever the subject comes up, is where most of the jobs are, anyway.

Boulder, in particular, seems to be an attractive place for startups, "one of the hottest places in the country to launch a company," according to a July 2010 story in *The Denver Post*. Boulder, with only about 6 percent of the state's total population, received 42 percent of the venture capital invested in Colorado from 2006 to 2009, the *Post* said. Boulder County also was home base for 8,900 businesses of fewer than twenty employees.

What works for Boulder also has worked for a number of growing companies around the region. There are plenty of small and midsize businesses based in Colorado, as well as some formerly modest companies that have grown into international presences. Software, biotechnology, natural foods, and anything associated with Colorado's outdoor lifestyle seem to thrive here. Some of them get big and then get bought by bigger competitors—Celestial Seasonings herbal teas, Alfalfa's organic grocers, and software innovator StorageTek are examples. But Boulder County still is home to Crocs, maker of those curious, ubiquitous, flexible shoes.

Governor Bill Ritter, soon after he took office in 2007, announced his commitment to making Colorado a leader in clean alternative energy development. Vestas, a manufacturer of wind turbines, was "one of Colorado's earliest visionaries and pioneers in our new energy economy," Ritter said at a March 2009 groundbreaking for one of several facilities the Danish company had planned for Colorado. A major draw in attracting such companies is the National Renewable Energy Laboratory in Golden, with its National Wind Technology Center south of Boulder.

Small Business in Colorado

When companies like Vestas and DaVita locate in Colorado, it attracts a lot of attention. But what's the environment like for small business? That depends a lot on who's answering the question. In the national economic burnout at the end of the new century's first decade, small businesses in Colorado were not faring much better than their counterparts elsewhere, said Tony Gagliardi, Colorado–Wyoming director of the National Federation of Independent Business (NFIB).

"One would be hard-pressed to say small business is booming in Colorado," Gagliardi said. What small business owners were telling him was "We simply do not have customers coming through the door," he said, and that hurt local spending as well as job creation. Expanded unemployment benefits also played a role, in Gagliardi's opinion, making it "easier for those trained in more specialized fields to be more selective in their job searches." Instead of going to work for a small business, these workers were waiting for an opening in their specialized field.

Wind turbines at the National Wind Technology Center, near Boulder. Photo courtesy of DOE/NREL, Patrick Corkery.

Tameka Montgomery, director of the Metro Denver Small Business Development Center (SBDC), agreed that the current economy was making everyone pay more attention to job security. But from her perspective, that meant they were more interested in trying to own their own businesses than in continuing to rely on large companies for a paycheck. "Small businesses are the creators of the net new jobs," she said. "They employ 51 percent of the work force."

Security for most small businesses includes having what Montgomery characterized as an "exit strategy." Eventually, the business owner is going to want to retire, or cash in on the investment he or she has made. There are four primary choices, Montgomery said: "1. Leadership is passed on to a family member; 2. An outside person is brought in to run the company; 3. Shut it down; or 4. Sell it."

And, she added, "For the small business owner, selling can be a really great option, considering the hard work invested to grow the business. The payoff can be great."

Gagliardi had a more pessimistic view. "In today's economy, one does not see many individuals able to purchase or willing to purchase a small business," he said. "Often times the exit strategy is simply closing the business."

Major Players Change

It's not just small businesses that change hands. The companies that dominate the Denver region today are a much different group than dominated, say, forty years ago. In 1970, for example, two of Denver's manufacturing giants were the Gates Corporation, which made tires, fan belts, hoses, and other rubber parts for motor vehicles of all sizes; and

Samsonite, formerly Shwayder Brothers, makers of a still-popular line of luggage as well as folding chairs and tables and, for a time, the US marketer for LEGO building blocks. In 1972, the rights to LEGO reverted back to the Danish inventors of the toy; in 1975, Samsonite sold to Beatrice Foods. Gates in 1996 became a wholly owned subsidiary of London-based Tomkins PLC, ending eighty-five years of ownership by the Gates family.

That was a different time in Denver and the Front Range. In 1970, the International Olympic Committee picked Denver as host city for the 1976 Winter Olympic Games, only to be rebuffed two years later by a statewide vote to deny state funding for the event. Currigan Hall convention center had opened in 1969, a big new venue with an exterior designed to rust. It was torn down in 2001 and replaced with an addition to the new Colorado Convention Center. There were fewer tall buildings downtown, though ambitious developers were planning to add a total of some 4 million square feet of office space over the next two to three years. IBM Selectric typewriters were the height of technology. Denver didn't yet have a Brooks Brothers outlet, though it did have several upscale local men's clothiers. You could fly from Denver to Honolulu and back for $375 round-trip on Western Airlines, and Braniff International was promising "a juicy steak for everyone on our lunch and dinner flights to Dallas/Fort Worth." Both airlines are now gone.

Some of the other big names in Denver business in 1970 have moved on, too. The savings and loan business is not what it used to be; the Public Service Company of Colorado is now Xcel Energy. Pentax

Solar Panels collecting energy near Boulder. Photo courtesy of DOE/NREL, Patrick Corkery.

still has its US headquarters in a Denver suburb, but it no longer is as impressive to the locals as it once was—not as much, say, as RE/MAX, whose real estate can be found as far away as Cape Town, South Africa; or MediaNews Group, the second-largest company of its type in the United States. The major players keep changing.

Businesses start, grow, sometimes dwindle, sometimes leave. It's not as though these sorts of transitions have hurt the region. They make for a livelier environment. Forty years ago, there weren't very many choices in Denver for really good food. The Brown Palace's restaurants could always be counted on for something a lot fancier than a smothered burrito, but most of the white-tablecloth places from those days are gone: the Qvorum, Top of the Rockies, Scotch 'n' Sirloin, Saltwater Dumas, The Library, the list goes on and on.

Now, though, there's a newer crop of trendy restaurants that have reputations for being healthy and innovative; there are microbreweries and wine bars and, interestingly, a whole subset of restaurants that illustrate how once-small businesses can become international. An unusually large number of "fast casual" restaurants are based in and around Denver, including fast-growing Chipotle, Quiznos, Noodles & Co., Boston Market, Qdoba, Good Times, Rock Bottom Brewery (including Old Chicago pizzerias), Tokyo Joe's, Smashburger, and what may be among the pioneers nationally in this segment, Village Inn, established in 1958.

The region is the home of other franchises, too, Tameka Montgomery pointed out—"a number of businesses that started here, are still located here and have had significant growth"—including Camp Bow Wow, 10 til 2 placement service, and Hyde Park Jewelers. Other companies that started small, got big, and stayed put include Namaste Solar and Eco-Products. Gagliardi's list of local success stories is based more on stability, including Denver Bookbinding, after seventy-five years the only bookbinding company left in Colorado; Centennial Container; and Alpine Credit Services.

In 2010, Colorado ranked third on CNBC's list of the best states in the country for doing business. The business news network cited quality of life, business friendliness, and strength of workforce. But Colorado also has disadvantages when compared with other states. Government budget limitations and open-meetings requirement, coupled with a fairly easy-to-access ballot process that makes it difficult to predict what new rules voters might enact, make it very difficult for the state to quietly negotiate the kind of economic incentives that other states are able to offer.

"The business leaders of Colorado can't just depend upon government to attract business but instead need to consciously get together and need to organize in a way that will allow us to efficiently go out and work our relationships and assist government in attracting business to Colorado," Ken Tuchman said in a 2010 interview with *The Denver Post*. Tuchman is chairman and chief executive of TeleTech, an outsourcing firm based in Douglas County with 43,000 employees around the world.

An Alternative to Incentives

The experts who advise companies on where to locate say the way to counter the short supply of incentive dollars is to support existing companies and help them grow—to produce good models that will attract the attention of new business. "A lot of clients are usually more interested in who's been there, how they've grown—not always the fluff story," said Michael Bennett, a site-election consultant at Jones Lang LaSalle. He was speaking at a meeting in Denver where the topic was economic development and expansion. In 2009 Don Marostica, Colorado's director of economic development, also said the key is to nurture existing businesses. "I want to make sure the companies we have, we're taking care of," Marostica said in a newspaper interview, "that we know six months before that Qwest is talking about merging so we can be figuring out how do we keep them here. We didn't know it."

Although he wasn't especially enthusiastic about the state's business climate in the midst of a stubborn economic slowdown, the NFIB's Gagliardi did have praise for what the Denver Metro Chamber is doing to support small business. "Many chambers of commerce face dilemmas in catering to small businesses," Gagliardi said. "Often the boards of directors are dominated by the largest employers and not actual small business owners. This can and often will create conflicts in the mission and objectives of the local chamber."

However, Gagliardi added, "I believe the Denver [Metro] Chamber does a good job of recognizing this fact and it is reflected in their programs available to members…Having the Denver Small Business Development Center housed in the Denver [Metro] Chamber by the [state] Office of Economic Development is a good resource to many individuals interested in starting their own business or expanding an existing business." He does wish, though, that state government and the legislature would recognize that small businesses are not just miniature versions of big companies. Laws affecting parental leave, employee insurance, and employer liability are harder for the owner of a small business to deal with, he said.

Among the ways the Denver Metro Chamber encourages the growth of small businesses, Montgomery said, are through its SBDC and the Small Business Transportation Resource Center. "I believe the key to encouraging entrepreneurism is having a support network where individual feel they can go to receive they help they need to become a successful and viable business," she said.

They start, they grow, and often they succeed—modestly or marvelously. And then they become just the sort of good examples the chamber can show off in its recruiting efforts. The chamber's Tom Clark pointed out that, in competition with Arizona and Texas, Denver wins the relocation decision more than half the time, rather than the third that raw numbers would suggest. In a state where big-dollar incentives and closed-door negotiations are all but impossible, those good examples are pivotal.

Denver, 1894

A panoramic view of Denver, Colorado, showing Sixteenth Street and the Arapahoe County Courthouse. Photo courtesy of the Denver Public Library Western History Collection, William Henry Jackson, WHJ-10367.

Chapter 5

Boom and Bust

Denver and Colorado have a history of good times followed by bad. The challenge for community leaders has always been to capitalize on the up years so the down years have less of an impact.

The waterways at Denver's heart are shallow, quirky, and a long way from anything approaching navigable. The confluence of Cherry Creek and the South Platte River makes for a fine park, however, and a fine place for an outing or a meeting. The area's indigenous inhabitants were well aware of that for decades before the first white pioneers arrived in the nineteenth century. It was there, too, that the first Anglo meeting of any significance was held. On November 17, 1858, a group of settlers gathered around a campfire they had built and, dodging the smoke and the popping sparks, decided to create a new township called Denver City. The site of their metropolitan dream was across the watercourses from two competitors—collections of tents, corrals, and bedrolls called St. Charles and Auraria.

Gold had drawn the white settlers, and word spread quickly. The tent city of Denver exploded with saloons, gambling halls, and wagon trains churning through the rutted streets—either dusty or muddy thoroughfares, depending on the recent weather. And where there's gold, a certain amount of lawlessness soon follows, especially where it's customary for male citizens to go about carrying firearms. In addition to the rough-hewn nature of the raw new place, in its first few years the city survived a flood, two major fires, several Indian attacks, and, during the Civil War, even raised a Union Army, defeating invading Confederates from Texas.

The flood of newcomers eventually—and with more than a little help from ambitious and avaricious nineteenth-century drafters of Indian treaties—drove the Arapaho from their traditional hunting and camping grounds.

An Early Transportation Campaign

The fledgling city, now a teenager, needed ways to communicate with the rest of the nation, and the world. It needed a railroad. But the Union Pacific was going to build its transcontinental line through Cheyenne, Wyoming, a hundred miles to the north. Not surprisingly, this was regarded as a great coup for Cheyenne. Westerners have never been slow to boast or to boost, and the people of Cheyenne were sure this sealed their chances for success and spelled Denver's doom to be something of a backwater.

It was only the first of several transportation struggles. Denver had to fight to be included in two intercontinental transportation routes: the railroads, in the nineteenth-century, and airmail and subsequent commercial air travel in the twentieth century. Almost exactly ten years after Denver City was dreamed up, on November 13, 1867, former territorial governor John Evans and newspaper publisher William N. Byers founded the Denver Board of Trade. Its principal concern was to bring a railroad to Denver, to avoid being left out.

John Evans became wealthy by investing in railroads, and he was celebrated as the founder of the Denver Seminary, which became the University of Denver. The town of Evanston, Illinois, where he was one of the founders of Northwestern University, also is named for him. So is Mount Evans, the 14,264-foot peak directly west of Denver. But he was far from a perfect role model. He had been forced

John Evans became wealthy by investing in growth in Denver. He even started a seminary that eventually became the University of Denver. Photo courtesy of the Denver Public Library Western History Collection, Z-2377.

from office in 1865 after a congressional investigation of the notorious Sand Creek Massacre, which Evans had ordered and later tried to downplay.

For his part, William N. Byers staked his claim to history by founding Denver's first newspaper as the boom was getting underway. The first *Rocky Mountain News* was published April 23, 1859, and survived the roller coaster of economic ups and downs for a century and a half. Unfortunately, the boomtown newspaper eventually fell victim to the worldwide economic bust of 2009 and ceased publication just weeks shy of its 150th anniversary.

The settlement at the confluence of creek and river grew slowly at first, but after Evans, Byers, and the Denver Board of Trade convinced the railroads to come through town, people poured in. Denver grew by 100,000 people between 1870 and 1890. Colorado became the 38th state in 1876, the centennial of the founding of the United States. Five years later, Denver beat out competitors Boulder, Colorado Springs, and Golden to become the state capital.

The boomtown experienced its first bust in 1893, after the price of silver plummeted and the value of all those mines was seriously devalued. Despite the decade of depression that followed, city leaders went on a building spree. The Colorado State Capitol building and the natural history museum, now called the Denver Museum of Nature and Science, were built during this period.

A New Century, a New Boom

As the twentieth century began, Denver started growing again. It wasn't the explosive growth of a few decades earlier, but it gave the city a more settled feeling. And then came Mayor Robert Speer, with a passion for urban planning and a blueprint that channeled the city's more stately growth along streets and near parks and shaded by more than 100,000 newly planted trees. Cherry Creek, still reeling from pollution left by early miners, was turned into an urban amenity, and new mountain parks were plotted out.

In 1918, the federal government decided to develop a transcontinental airmail route. "Once again, Cheyenne was picked as a stopover rather than Denver," Jeff Miller wrote in his history of Stapleton Airport. The reasoning was the same: the mountains west of Denver were too high. But, similar to what happened with the nineteenth-century railroads, Denver would wind up with a north-south feeder airmail route, with stops in Pueblo, Denver, and Cheyenne.

In 1929, Ben Stapleton, then the Denver mayor, decided to build an airport. It was called "Stapleton's Folly" by its detractors, just as today's DIA came to be known as "Peña's Folly." Critics said—and this will sound familiar to anyone who has followed the DIA story—that Stapleton's airport was so far east of the settled parts of the city that "it might as well be in Kansas." But the scorn didn't last long.

Almost from the beginning, Stapleton was one of the nation's busiest airports. During the 1930s and 1940s, drawn in part by the city's emergence as a transportation hub, the US government picked Denver for Lowry Air Force Base and the Denver Federal Center. Those and other installations that followed give Denver the largest population of federal employees after Washington, DC.

Stapleton International Airport, with Denver to the West. Photo courtesy of the Denver Public Library Western History Collection.

Following World War II, the city boomed again, doubling in population by 1960. Military personnel who had been stationed here, or maybe just passed through, wanted to return to make it a permanent home. Some things came almost out of the blue, but still would not have happened without aggressive local leadership being prepared to move quickly when the opportunities presented themselves. In the middle of the twentieth century, the US Air Force Academy came to Colorado. Temporarily housed at Lowry Air Force Base in Denver, it soon moved to a spectacular campus north of Colorado Springs. That same year, in 1954, the Department of Commerce located a new National Bureau of Standards laboratory in Boulder, and other research-oriented facilities weren't far behind. The I. M. Pei–designed Mile High Center opened in downtown Denver during that year, 1954, of almost unprecedented growth.

Natural resources firms increasingly chose Denver to be their regional or national headquarters. Oil companies from around the world flocked to the city and began changing its skyline. Buildings of forty, fifty, and more stories sprang up under the booms of constantly pivoting aerial cranes. As Americans enjoyed more leisure time, Denver profited from the growth in tourism—especially skiing. The energy boom of the 1970s also produced rapid growth in Denver's suburbs, including a slightly smaller version of downtown in the Denver Tech Center office park southeast of the city core.

Denver's boomtown reputation was international, thanks in no small part to a popular television series called *Dynasty*. The saga of the wealthy Carrington family aired for eight years, from 1981 to 1989, through the rise and the fall of Denver's fortunes. Just as silver's decline in value precipitated a crash a century earlier, a plunge in the price of oil triggered another down time in Denver. The price of a barrel of oil went from $39 to just $9, and the air went out of the region's balloon. Many of the oil companies left, as did the other workers who made their livings from the resources boom. The glittering skyscrapers went largely empty.

GDC to the Rescue

In the late 1980s, the Greater Denver Corporation was formed by Denver's chamber of commerce to stimulate economic revival, attract new development and promote government policies that helped toward those ends. Over the GDC's eight-year lifespan, it raised more than $14 million, won two major infrastructure elections, and successfully lobbied for legislation that helped the region recover from its economic malaise. "In my view," former *Denver Post* editor William Hornby wrote in his 1995 retrospective on the GDC, "Denver's civic leadership quite often has a special disdain for failure and a special faith in aggressive private enterprise. Both disdain of failure and faith in enterprise were born of the gold prospecting ethic of the city's birth, and of its frontier-spawned instinct to meet crisis head-on as a matter of sheer survival...Enthusiastic and boastful private enterprise birthed Denver."

The formation of the GDC heralded a new attitude. Metropolitan area communities stopped competing for new business and amenities and started working together. The cooperation came from a realization that it made no sense for Aurora to have its own zoo, or for Golden to have a major symphony orchestra, or Littleton to have an NFL team competing with the Broncos. People living in a metropolitan area, and especially those visiting from elsewhere, see all of these clustered cultural, entertainment, and corporate attractions as part of the same civic amenity package.

As former chamber president Richard C. D. Fleming put it in a 1992 interview:

> The world sees Denver as you see it from an airplane—without artificial boundaries. We should treat it that way and deal together with the common problems of air pollution, economic development, transportation and water. We need to market Denver as a six-county metropolis and let prospects see all the alternatives. That's a lot better than having each country try to build itself us by running down the others.

The GDC was launched in February, holding its first board meeting on October 12, 1987, and it carried out its mission through 1995. It seems fair to call it a success. GDC members worked aggressively to attract a healthy mix of new industries to Denver, diversifying the heavy reliance on natural resources that had brought the city to a low point in the middle of the decade of the 1980s. The oil and gas business, which had employed an estimated 28,500 people in Denver in 1982, by 1988 had lost half those jobs. Federico Peña first was elected Denver's mayor in 1983, at a low point in the city's fortunes, but his optimistic campaign slogan, Imagine a Great City, captured where the electorate wanted to go. He was reelected in 1987, the year the GDC came into being. Earlier that year, the Colorado Association of Commerce and Industry, a statewide economic development group, published its "Blueprint for Colorado—A Plan for Growth from the Business Community." One of the major recommendations in the "Blueprint" was to build a new airport by the early 1990s, a goal to which the new GDC also devoted a considerable share of its financial resources.

Denver mayor Frederico Peña served two terms, from 1983 to 1991. Photo courtesy of the Denver Public Library Western History Collection.

Over its nine-year life, the GDC worked to bring a number of new developments to the region, including a few that got away. But it devoted its energies, and contributed money, to campaigns for a light-rail line, a new convention center, new football and baseball stadiums, extension of the Scientific and Cultural Facilities District, Denver annexation of airport land in Adams County, and a Denver vote affirming the airport decision. The Denver Metro Chamber sent teams of "Denvoys" around the world to talk to business executives about relocating. The "Denvoys" were disbanded when their business practices became too lax. By early 1990, the chamber had hosted 270 executives from 150 different corporations at a dozen site-selection conferences. It worked with airlines to give Denver travelers access to international cities.

The GDC spawned an extraordinary, widely praised coalition of regional municipal governments and business groups called the Metro Denver Network (MDN). It was announced in February 1987, created by an intergovernmental agreement signed by governor Roy Romer and mayors and other officials from twenty different cities, including Denver mayor Federico Peña and Aurora mayor Paul Tauer, whose cities had a history of fierce competition.

The MDN had a Code of Ethics, founded, it said, "on the mutual respect and trust of its members." Among its provisions were that members "shall endeavor to sell metro Denver first and our individual communities second." It dedicated itself to fair competition and new partnerships and declared, "At no time shall any member of the Network knowingly compete for a fellow member's prospects without notification or communication between the members unless the prospect specifically requests otherwise."

In his 1993 book, *Citistates—How Urban America Can Prosper in a Competitive World,* urban affairs columnist Neal Pierce lauded the Denver area's experience as an example of how cities drive the economic fortunes of entire regions. Pierce wrote,

> For concerted region-wide economic planning, few communities have matched the so-called Metro Denver Network (MDN)...Virtually every chamber and economic development agency in the Denver metropolitan region—53 at last count—signed on to the network, even though many of the counties and municipalities had a history of abrasive relations. The effort amounts to the United States' first region-wide, computerized information system to track every new business lead and all available sites, and to provide unified national advertising and coordinated screening of industrial prospects. Begun in 1987, in the pits of a regional recession, the Network by 1992 was claiming some credit for a strong economic turnaround in the region and creation of some 100,000 new jobs.

The MDN was designed to outlast the GDC, pursuing its ideals for decades to come. In a way, though, it became a victim of its own success. FutureWorks, a consulting firm that studies regional economic development efforts, had this assessment: "The boom and prosperity of the 1990s contributed to contentment and the Metro Denver Network's programs were supported half-heartedly. In 2002, with another economic crisis underway, economic development officials and business leaders criticized the chamber for letting the Metro Denver Network falter." The chamber responded by hiring Tom Clark—again—in 2003, this time to oversee the activities of the new Metro Denver EDC.

The 1990s—Booming Again

During Peña's two terms as mayor, from 1983 to 1991, the "great city" spirit manifested itself at the polls—and not just in Denver, but regionally. In addition to the two elections giving the go-ahead on the airport, regional voters approved a tenth-of-a-percent sales tax to support regional cultural attractions in 1988, and then in 1990 a similar amount to build a baseball stadium. When that tax expired, the voters agreed to extend it for a new football stadium. In the city of Denver itself, voters approved a $242 million bond issue to pave streets, redevelop the South Platte Valley, spruce up the parks, restore Civic Center Park and the City and County Building, and update Denver General Hospital and the National Western Stock Show, Rodeo, and Horse Show complex.

The $126 million Colorado Convention Center, since expanded, was completed in 1990. And remember, the city was still pulling out ever so slowly from the greatest depression since the Great Depression sixty years earlier. Voters that same year approved spending $200 million in bonds on Denver Public Schools, and $95 million more to improve and enlarge the library system, including adding to the central library.

In that same decade came three major regional shopping centers: Park Meadows Mall south of the core city, FlatIron Crossing to the north, and Cherry Creek Shopping Center close to downtown. All of them—Cherry Creek in particular—feature high-end shopping that had never been available in the state before. New residential space was developed in and near downtown. The former Stapleton airport became a diversified, multiple-use, thoroughly integrated residential, commercial, and business development.

But not every attempt at development was received warmly. After Denver finally won a long-sought bid to host the 1976 Winter Olympics, former Governor Richard Lamm, then a state representative, raised environmental concerns and led a citizen initiative campaign to deny state funding to support the games. The vote was in 1972, and more than 59 percent of Coloradans agreed with him. Lamm's work on that campaign laid the foundation for his successful run for governor in 1974. He always was perceived as antigrowth, but that didn't hurt his high approval ratings or stop him from being reelected twice by large margins.

Regional voters also were skeptical about an early attempt at mass transit development called Guide the Ride, rejecting it at the polls. A proposal to build Two Forks Dam and Reservoir, southwest of Denver in a mountain canyon, was earnestly sought by local developers and officials but strenuously opposed by environmentalists and was at the center of a divisive controversy among local residents. After decades of debate, in 1990 the Environmental Protection Agency denied the permit that would have allowed the dam to be built.

There have been other lost causes, too. In 1991, when United Airlines was looking for a site to build a new maintenance center, when the US government was looking for a place for a massive experimental project called the Superconducting Super Collider, and again in 1998 when Boeing sought to move its corporate headquarters from Seattle, the entire state legislature got behind efforts to offer incentives. But the state's open meetings laws may have gotten in the way. Colorado law doesn't permit closed-door negotiations, except for strictly limited purposes. Boeing went to Chicago instead of Denver; Indianapolis got the maintenance center;

Confluence Park, so named because Cherry Creek and the South Platte River converge at this site. This is where Denver began in 1859. Photo © 2011 Willie Gibson.

and Waxahachie, Texas, was chosen as the home of the Superconducting Super Collider. The Collider, though, was never built, and the maintenance center in Indianapolis has been largely abandoned and converted to other uses.

When projects have succeeded, it's because voters have been convinced of a need. Despite earlier failures of transportation plans, regional voters approved a multimodal approach called FasTracks in 2002, including new lanes of interstate highway as well as a 119-mile extension of the light-rail system, more than triple its existing size. In Denver in 2007, voters approved each and every one of an ambitious eleven proposals for infrastructure improvements backed by the city's popular mayor, John Hickenlooper. None of these would have succeeded without business and government leaders working together effectively in convincing the public, and with an understanding of the community's history, assets, and goals—what University of Colorado professor Susan E. Clarke calls the community's "story." As she told a National League of Cities Conference in 2005, "Articulating this story publicly and persuasively is a key role for leaders."

Over the decade of the 1990s, the city of Denver's population grew by 30 percent. People from all walks of life have made Denver their home, creating a city diverse in culture and opportunities. Today, the metropolitan area's population is approaching 3 million, and Denver remains the largest urban center in a vast and scenic, but overall sparsely populated, quarter of the country. With the support of the entire metropolitan area, it has made investments that allowed the region to face the worldwide economic recession of 2009 equipped with several new tools that have helped it weather the downturn. There was indeed another downturn, a bust to follow another boom—businesses closed, or moved. But the area represented by the Denver Metro Chamber of Commerce has "incredible strengths," said chamber president and CEO Kelly J. Brough. "We remain incredibly competitive out there."

Denver, 1913

Northwestward view of downtown Denver taken from the dome of the State Capitol, at the intersection of Lincoln Street and Colfax Avenue. Photo courtesy of the Denver Public Library Western History Collection, L. C. McClure, MCC-2274.

Chapter 6

Making a Mark in Sports and Culture

All work and no play would make Denver a dull burg, or in the phrase often used affectionately by its residents, just another dusty old cow town. But with the business community's enthusiastic support, the metropolitan area has become a leading example of how to use regional cooperation to attract big-league sports and support first-class cultural institutions.

The Scientific and Cultural Facilities District (SCFD) was an innovation, a precedent-setting way of supporting the arts that showed the region's willingness to work together—and not just at the leadership level, but at the grassroots level where the voters could make their wishes known.

The economic downturn of the early 1980s represented a serious financial problem for the Denver region and its cultural attractions. In 1982, the state legislature ended direct state support for four major regional attractions: the Denver Art Museum, the Denver Botanic Gardens, the Denver Museum of Natural History (now the Denver Museum of Nature and Science), and the Denver Zoo. The city of Denver continued its financial support, but visitors to the "Big Four" were charged an admission fee for the first time.

Six years later, in 1988, the legislature agreed to seek voter approval of a tax to support cultural and scientific attractions. It wasn't much—0.1 percent, or a penny on every $10 sale—and voters apparently thought it was a small price to pay. The level of popular support was remarkable; the ballot issue creating the district and enacting the tax passed by 75 percent overall, and the lowest margin of approval in any of the six metro area counties involved in the district was 2 to 1 in Adams County.

The district now includes a seventh entity, the City and County of Broomfield, which used to be part of three counties until it restructured itself in 2001.

Political consultant Floyd Ciruli, who ran an imaginative pro-SCFD campaign for the trustees of the Big Four institutions, said the business community wasn't particularly involved in that first effort. Business interests, and the Denver Metro Chamber in particular, were "almost entirely consumed at that time with the new airport." The idea that cultural attractions had considerable economic benefits "really wasn't in common play at that time," Ciruli said. The chamber did, however, contribute $50,000 to buy media advertising in September 1988, two months before the election.

The election showed how much support this precedent-setting idea had, and by the time the SCFD tax was up for renewal in 1994, the chamber's enthusiasm had grown. By the next renewal vote, in 1994, the SCFD and the organizations it supported had "become one of the major interests of business, including this chamber," Ciruli said. "They have evolved into it." In the run-up to the 2004 election, in 2001 and 2002, "they became totally supportive and quite active," Ciruli said. In November 2004, the vote to continue taxpayer support for culture was 65 percent in favor. The tax is now due to continue until June 30, 2018, but there will be another renewal vote before then.

As the Colorado Business Committee for the Arts (CBCA) points out in its 2008 study of economic impact of cultural attractions, "Museums, zoos and theaters are businesses. They employ dancers, musicians, craftspeople, auditors, consultants and maintenance workers. They improve our quality of life and entertain, but also spend money, create jobs and offer educational opportunities for all. They are valuable and indispensable."

In 2007, the CBCA reported, the total regional economic activity attributable to the arts reached close to $1.7 billion, a 19 percent increase over the previous study period in 2005. In 2007, the organizations comprising the SCFD employed 8,244 people at a total payroll of more than $119 million. They also benefited from the services of nearly 40,000 volunteers. The institutions contributed some $21.3 million in combined payroll, seat, and sales taxes for 2007. "The arts are part of everyday life here for people of all ages and backgrounds," the CBCA said. "Cultural and scientific organizations enjoyed over 16.4 million total visits in 2007 (17 percent more than in

The Denver Center for the Performing Arts. Photo © 2011 ewingphoto.com.

2005). This equates to six arts events per resident of the seven-county area!"

The Denver Center for the Performing Arts was the dream of the late owner of *The Denver Post*, Helen G. Bonfils, and the brainchild of Donald M. Seawell, a lawyer and Broadway producer. The first piece of the 12-acre complex, the 2,700-seat Boettcher Concert Hall, opened in 1978. In 2007, former University of Denver chancellor Daniel L. Ritchie succeeded Seawell as chairman of the complex. It's the second-largest complex of its kind in the country. Bond elections funding improvements to the complex—and to the Denver Zoo, the Denver Public Library system, and other core-city attractions—also have been supported by the Denver Metro Chamber over the years.

In Ciruli's assessment, the chamber has become increasingly progressive over the years, shunning the antitax, antigovernment attitude associated with what chambers of commerce used to stand for. Cultural attractions, sports venues—"All of these things involved either taxes or major changes in land use," Ciruli said—yet they had enthusiastic support from the Denver Metro Chamber of Commerce.

The Old Ball Game(s)

Building on the cultural district prototype, regional voters approved another small sales tax to build a new stadium for major-league baseball and then agreed to extend that tax to build a new football stadium. Denver today fields major-league teams in football, baseball, basketball, and hockey, and major contenders in soccer, lacrosse, and other sports. It's the smallest metropolitan area, at something short of 3 million people, with all of the "big four." But for years, baseball—the sport of legend, of grassy fields, lazy summer leisure hours, and fanatic poring over statistics—had been an elusive dream. The minor-league Denver Bears were fun, but they just weren't big league. Over the years, several attempts had been made to bring the bigs to Denver, but none of them succeeded. But when Major League Baseball decided in 1989 to add two franchises, beginning in just four years, Denver wanted to be first in line.

It was going to take another public-private partnership to succeed, and the state legislature had to be convinced to refer the tax question to voters. That campaign—or campaigns, since both legislature and voters had to be convinced—is described more thoroughly in the chapter that follows, but for now suffice it to say that it worked. After a slow start, with polls showing the public opposed 2 to 1, the tax issue eventually passed on August 14, 1990, by a fairly comfortable margin of 54 to 46 percent.

Less than a year later, MLB owners awarded new franchises to Denver and Miami. Ground for Coors Field was broken at Twentieth and Blake streets in downtown Denver in September 1992, and the stadium opened in time for the beginning of the 1995 baseball season. Coors Field, built in a nostalgic style with lots of bricks and exposed girders, was a hit. New restaurants and offices were drawn to it, bringing a new vibrancy to downtown Denver.

Coors Field also proved to be a moneymaker. Denver's economy was improving, and it was clear that the stadium's bonds would be paid off well before the original twenty-year expiration date for the tax, which was set for 2012. Bond rates were down, sales tax revenues were up, and the Denver Broncos saw an opportunity. Chamber leader M. Doak Jacoway was playing golf with Pat Bowlen in 1995 when the Broncos owner told him he needed a new stadium to replace Mile High Stadium if the team was to continue to be competitive. Bowlen didn't go public with that wish until after the Broncos won their first Super Bowl, in 1998.

In 1999, the Broncos owner, represented by longtime lobbyist Bill Artist, asked the state legislature to approve extending the tax to pay for a new football stadium. Colorado's legislature, of course, can't raise taxes on its own; it can only ask voters to approve. It didn't hurt that the Broncos had just won their second Super Bowl victory in two years, but even so, it was a close vote by which the legislature approved putting the issue to metro area voters. The campaign, Jacoway said, had to be based on blue-collar fans, and Bowlen and Mayor Webb both had to stay pretty much in the background; neither was very popular among that grassroots base. Telling them to stay out of the spotlight "was not an easy conversation to have," Jacoway recalled.

Artist ran the CFANS campaign (Citizens for a New Stadium), raising $1.8 million of the $3 million spent in the winning effort. Much of the support came from Denver's business community. Bowlen had hinted that the Broncos might move to Los Angeles or Houston or some other city desperate for a franchise unless the team had a new stadium in Denver. But he was the largest single contributor to the stadium campaign, at $1.2 million. He and other stadium supporters, including many members of the Denver Metro Chamber, spent $2.3 million on advertising and lobbying. The popular vote wasn't nearly as close as the legislative vote, by electoral standards. The tax extension was approved by a margin of 57 to 43 percent, 6 percentage points more than the approval for the original baseball tax. The baseball-football tax still is set to expire on or before 2012, but indications so far are that the deadline won't be a problem.

Extending the tax to cover football "was a comparatively easy sell," said Gail Klapper, who was chair of the Denver Metro Chamber at the time of the vote. "People said, 'OK, I'm already paying that. It hasn't killed me. And we're getting something great.'" It was another example, in an uncertain economic climate, of convincing voters to make "an investment at a time investment was difficult," she said.

There was considerable controversy over what the new stadium was to be called. Football fans, who tend to be loyal and resistant to change, were attached to the name Mile High Stadium. Then mayor Wellington Webb wasn't keen about selling naming rights, even though it could mean removing close to $90 million of the debt for building the $400 million stadium. Invesco, an investment management company that few Denverites knew much about, successfully bid $120 million for the naming rights. John Hickenlooper, then a restaurant owner but soon to be Denver's mayor, was one of the leaders of the campaign to keep the old name, and there are those who think his folksy appeal was the beginning of a successful political career. As a bit of a compromise, the stadium ended up with the official name of Invesco Field

The uppermost levels of the Daniels and Fisher Tower, with Invesco Field in the background. Photo © 2011 ewingphoto.com.

at Mile High. For a time *The Denver Post* refused to use the new name, but eventually popular usage came to be simply Invesco Field.

Invesco Field is a little bit removed from the other attractions in Denver's Central Platte Valley, but it's still part of a complex of new downtown attractions that has reinvigorated the area where the city got its start a century and a half ago. From Coors Field on the north to Elitch Gardens and the Pepsi Center on the south, the right bank of the South Platte River has become a magnet for downtown visitors. Both Elitch's, as longtime Denverites prefer to call it, and the Pepsi Center were built with private money. The amusement park relocated from its historic site a couple of miles northwest of downtown. The $180 million Pepsi Center opened in late 1999 after a twenty-one-month building project, replacing the city-owned McNichols Arena. The Pepsi Center was host to the 2008 Democratic National Convention, the first national party nominating convention to be held in Denver since the Democrats met in the city one hundred years previously, in 1908.

Speaking of Conventions...

It may not have had the same level of attention or been considered in the same elevated realm of significance as DIA or the Metro Denver Network, but the building of a new convention center in Denver also was considered a major economic development priority.

Denver's existing convention center, Currigan Hall, had opened barely twenty years previously, but it wasn't big enough to attract the kinds of big conventions that were going to other cities. Currigan, named after former

The Ferris wheel at Elitch Gardens amusement park. Photo © 2011 Greg Thow.

The Pepsi Center, which replaced the aging city-owned McNichols Arena, was host to the 2008 Democratic National Convention. Photo © 2011 Willie Gibson.

Denver mayor Tom Currigan, was literally going to rust—but intentionally so. It had been built in 1969 with a type of steel whose oxidation was considered a decorative element. It had 100,000 gross square feet on two floors—large enough for boat shows and auto shows and state political party conventions, but not for meetings of tens of thousands of people. Denver was losing those to larger meeting halls elsewhere. So once again city officials and business leaders responded.

"The Convention Center was the confidence-builder" for working on other efforts to increase Denver's ability to draw crowds, said M. Doak Jacoway, a former chamber chairman. Discussion about building a new convention center had begun well before the chamber decided to coalesce its economic development efforts around the Greater Denver Corporation. But once the GDC was on hand to help, its contributions were key to the success of the effort.

A convention center was one of Mayor Peña's goals in the mid-1990s (the Newspaper Guild's satirical Gridiron Show referred to it as the "Hall o' Peña). The mayor's preferred site was behind Union Station in the rapidly reviving Platte Valley. But that proposed site was defeated in a 1985 election, leaving the mayor and the city council sharply divided on the issue. City planners and developers weren't keen about the existing Currigan Hall site, but it seemed to have popular support.

There is educational value in any campaign, even a losing one. Supporters of a new site as well as the public learned more about the benefits and problems of various locations around the Downtown area. And the fight hadn't hurt

The Michael Graves–designed Denver Public Library, central branch, opened in 1995 and is the largest library between Los Angeles and Chicago. Photo © 2011 ewingphoto.com

the mayor too much politically; he was reelected in 1987. His reelection set off a new round of discussions. Denver developers Sam Gary and Al Cohen came up with a plan to build a meeting venue just south of the Denver Public Library, a location referred to as the Civic Center–Golden Triangle site. Denver billionaire Phil Anschutz proposed another location, in the Platte Valley, roughly where the Pepsi Center ended up.

Complicating the discussions was the fact that Denver was short of money, and it had asked the state legislature for financial help—specifically, $36 million to buy land. The city's argument was that a convention center would help the entire state by attracting more tourist traffic. Conventioneers would bring their families and spend a few extra days visiting, touring the sights in the rest of the state. That's why it's called the Colorado

Convention Center, and not the Denver Convention Center.

Anschutz had gone directly to the legislature. Gary and Cohen had gotten backing from the mayor and council first, but the legislature wasn't keen on their proposed location only a couple of blocks from the Capitol. And some legislators, especially those from outside the metropolitan area, saw no reason to pour millions into what they figured was just a project that would help mainly Denver. The Eastern Plains weren't likely to see much benefit from that vaunted tourist traffic.

All this squabbling was taking place as the GDC was just starting up, and it was one of the GDC's first political challenges. It and the chamber put the convention center high on their priority list and allocated $250,000 to win the legislative battle for land acquisition

The 146,000-square-foot Frederic C. Hamilton Building of the Denver Art Museum, designed by Daniel Libeskind, was opened to the public in 2006. The building is covered in 9,000 titanium panels to reflect the Colorado sunshine. Photo © 2011 ewingphoto.com.

funding. That effort succeeded, but the legislature—in addition to insisting that the new complex bear the name of the entire state—also required that an outside expert be brought in to pick a site. The GDC stepped up to the plate again, arranging for the Urban Land Institute to broker the dispute.

Eventually the feuding parties were won over to a third site, developer David French's proposal to build adjacent to the existing Currigan Hall in an area referred to as the Silver Triangle. It didn't become the favorite, though, until the Urban Land Institute declared it to be the best compromise—and the chamber, and the GDC, kept their pledge to abide by the third-party arbitration process. In his history of the GDC, Bill Hornby called the convention center battle "the GDC's first major test by fire, and it came through successful—though slightly singed."

The Colorado Convention Center, with more than 1 million square feet of exhibition and meeting space, opened in 1990. But the city still was losing out to larger venues. In November 1999, Denver voters approved issuing bonds to expand the still comparatively new venue. An expanded Colorado Convention Center opened in 2005. With 2.2 million square feet, it's still only the fifteenth largest convention center in the country. But it has spectacular views from its towering glass walls, and the big blue bear with its back to California Street, a 40-foot-tall statue entitled *I See What You Mean* that seems to peer in at convention-goers, is one of Denver's most-photographed attractions.

Other Achievements

During the decade that began with the convention center battle and ended with the opening of DIA, the chamber and the GDC were busily reaching out to pick some other plums. These projects weren't as highly visible or as controversial, but they were other examples of energetic efforts dedicated to getting the region out of its economic doldrums.

As the nation, and the world, entered another economic slump—this one the most serious in decades—some of the projects the chamber and its subdivisions helped bring to Colorado have been forced to make layoffs to make ends meet. But at least they're a diverse group of companies, a healthier state of affairs than what happened a quarter century earlier, when so much of the region's fortunes were tied to the fate of the natural resources industries.

Among the "gets" have been Kodak Colorado, which broke ground in Windsor in 1969 and only recently

SCFD vote 1988 by county

	% yes	% no
Adams	67.5	32.5
Arapahoe	76.2	23.8
Boulder	74.6	25.4
Denver	76.1	23.9
Douglas	77.9	22.1
Jefferson	74.6	25.4

The overall vote was 74.5 percent in favor to 25.5 percent against; almost 3 to 1 in favor. Only Adams County was just a little bit reluctant.

SCFD renewal 2004 by county

	% yes	% no
Adams	53.3	46.7
Arapahoe	66.3	33.7
Boulder	68.5	31.5
Broomfield	64.0	36.0
Denver	73.9	26.1
Douglas	62.3	37.7
Jefferson	64.9	35.1

The overall vote was 65.9 percent in favor to 34.1 percent against; a slight drop-off in support from the original election setting up the district.

T-REX bond approval 1999 by county

	% yes	% no
Adams	43.8	56.2
Arapahoe	73.6	26.4
Boulder	65.1	34.9
Denver	72.9	27.1
Douglas	76.4	23.6
Jefferson	60.7	39.3

The total vote was almost 2 to 1 in favor, 65.6 percent to 34.4 percent. Only Adams County voted against funding the project.

closed to cut back after a period of expansion. Johns Manville moved its world headquarters from New York to Denver in 1971. The chamber and the GDC helped bring a Merrill Lynch division to Lakewood. Up With People, a youth motivational program, left Tucson, Arizona, in 1995 to set up a new headquarters in Broomfield. The United Launch Alliance, engineering rockets at its facility in Waterton Canyon, provides the operating systems for some of the nation's most fascinating space-age experiments.

A somewhat unexpected boon was the decision of ConocoPhillips to buy the former StorageTek campus in Louisville in 2008 to develop clean-energy systems such as hydrogen fuel cells, solar and wind power, and diesel fuel made from renewable resources. These are examples of the areas identified by the Denver Metro Chamber of Commerce and the Metro Denver EDC as prime prospects for growth. The seven areas are aerospace, aviation, bioscience, broadcasting and telecommunications, conventional and alternative energy, financial services, and information technology and software.

The chamber also continues to place major emphasis on multimodal transportation. An early effort was a $150,000 loan to support a proposed Transit Construction Authority in 1988. The authority, which failed to get legislative support,

FasTracks vote 2004 by county		
	% yes	% no
Adams	47.1	52.9
Arapahoe	56.1	43.9
Boulder	64.4	35.6
Broomfield	53.9	46.1
Denver	65.2	34.8
Douglas	56.0	44.0
Jefferson	56.0	44.0
Weld	50.2	49.8

The total vote was 57.9 percent in favor, 42.1 percent against. Only Adams County was against the idea. A very small part of Weld County was included in the district, where the issue passed by only five votes.

was to consider rapid transit from downtown to the Denver Tech Center. It was succeeded, though, by the T-REX Project, a combination of freeway widening and light-rail expansion. T-REX (TRansportation EXpansion) was a major chamber goal, and it has proven to be very popular with commuters since it was completed—under budget and almost two years ahead of schedule—in 2006. A further expansion of light-rail, called FasTracks, was endorsed by 58 percent of the region's voters in 2004. Tax revenue hasn't lived up to expectations, though, and some local governments complain that promises aren't being kept in a timely way. But there are some hopeful signs, and construction is continuing.

Beyond infrastructure, the chamber is tackling some public policy issues as well. It remains committed to fighting extreme antitax, antigovernment amendments, and to reform the process by which those initiatives get on the ballot. The chamber's members are of a conservative bent, but they realize—as we'll see in a later chapter—that public-private partnerships won't work if the public part of the partnership is demoralized and underfunded.

Denver, 1930–1933

View looking northwest from the dome of the Colorado State Capitol. Photo courtesy of the Denver Public Library Western History Collection, L. C. McClure, MCC-3057A.

Chapter 7
Outgrowing Stapleton

Denver's Stapleton International Airport, often ranked among the five busiest in the country, was getting to be a problem. Residents living nearby were worried about noise and safety. When the wind was from the east, as it often was, huge jetliners would roar over leafy Montview Boulevard as they approached Stapleton's runways, their landing gear and soot-streaked bellies looming what seemed to be just a few hundred feet above backyard barbecues, bicycle riders, and families visiting the Denver Zoo. As the years went by, the airport got even busier and the planes got even bigger.

As early as the 1970s, people were beginning to talk about building a new airport, recalls Bob Albin, the energetic father of the campaign to do something about Stapleton. The original city airport, which opened in 1929, was about to reach the half century mark. It had been added to over the years, its concourses stretching out in several directions like a spider's legs. Air traffic had increased markedly. The runways were too close together to permit two aircraft to land side-by-side in bad weather, and delays in Denver were affecting air travel across the nation. It was time to examine the long-term survivability of Stapleton, Albin said. "By the turn of the century, we had to drastically expand or completely replace the existing airport."

The Denver Regional Council of Governments produced a Regional Airport System Plan in 1974. The area studied by San Francisco–based consultants Peat, Marwick, Mitchell & Co. for possible airport sites extended 30 miles north and 40 miles east of the city, a total of 1,230 square miles. Stapleton, some 7 miles from the center of downtown, was one of the nation's closest-in major airports, second behind only Miami. Regional travelers, except perhaps for the airport's close-in neighbors, were happy with that arrangement. The study found that "both air travelers and the public would prefer expansion of Stapleton International Airport. On the other hand, communities near the Airport would prefer that the Airport be moved to another location." That pretty much framed the dilemma that would confront airport planners for the next thirty years.

Four years later, in 1978, Albin and the Denver Metro Chamber invited more than fifty business leaders to participate in a committee to study the potential need to replace Stapleton. That was the same year the federal government deregulated the commercial air travel industry, and the nature of air travel changed. Denver benefited more than most places, as three airlines—Frontier, Continental, and United—chose to

A crowded Stapleton International Airport. Photo courtesy of the Denver Public Library Western History Collection.

make it a hub in their new hub-and-spoke systems. Delays continued to be a problem, though. In 1985, Western Airlines, now defunct, ran an ad in *The Wall Street Journal* to promote its Salt Lake City hub. The illustration was of a harried businessman entering a boardroom and announcing: "Sorry I'm late. I had to fly through Denver."

Regardless of how deregulation and hubs might change airline operations, the region's leaders still were convinced that there would continue to be transportation opportunities that could be used to good advantage. "Denver was a pretty sleepy town then," Albin recalled. After a year of study, in 1979 the committee recommended having a new airport in place by the turn of the century—still more than twenty years in the future. The committee enlisted the support of the Denver Regional Council of Governments (DRCOG), which already had gone on record as being interested in a new airport. The regional team went to the Federal Aviation Administration, which also was hoping to find a way to solve the bottleneck that Stapleton was creating system-wide whenever the Colorado weather was less than idyllic for aircraft operations. Denver and the FAA commissioned DRCOG to do further exploration of specific sites for a new airport.

Amidst all of this studying and pondering and yearning for an updated airport, in 1981, four families in Denver's Park Hill neighborhood, which lies under the eastbound approach to Stapleton, and one family in Montbello, northeast of the old airport, brought a lawsuit seeking relief from the noise and the threat of airplanes crashing into their homes. The lawsuit added urgency to the talk of building a new airport and offered strong evidence that the current airport's closest neighbors weren't as fond of it as a lot of the rest of the region. If the homeowners' lawsuit were to succeed, Stapleton very well might be forced to close. But it never got to that point. A settlement finally was negotiated in 1985, with Mayor Peña agreeing that a new airport would be built and Stapleton closed by 2000, and that the old airport would never again be used for "aeronautical activity." Peña now thinks that provision was "the hidden jewel of the compromise," because the redevelopment of the abandoned airport into the mixed-use, racially diverse Stapleton neighborhood has "gone very well."

In 1982, after nearly four years of study by elected officials, community leaders and airline executives, the

DRCOG recommended expanding Stapleton onto Rocky Mountain Arsenal. Everyone was in agreement. Or almost everyone. There was one important exception: Adams County wanted no part of Arsenal expansion. "Adams County raised all kinds of hell about it. And they said 'Over our dead body will you ever put an airport in Adams County,'" Albin said.

Study After Study

Once it got underway, the drive to replace Stapleton was proceeding along many fronts, and taking a number of directions. Early on, the most logical course of action appeared to be to expand the existing airport's runways, and probably build a newer terminal, using the soon-to-be-abandoned site occupied by Rocky Mountain Arsenal. The arsenal had been used until 1957 as a manufacturing site for chemical weapons, chiefly nerve gas. Those deadly compounds continued to be stored there, and up until around 1970, part of arsenal operations consisted of filling artillery shells with the toxic stuff. The air force also made rocket fuel on the arsenal site, and Shell Chemical Co. manufactured pesticides on land it leased from the army until about 1987. It was a nastily contaminated piece of land. One early effort to dispose of contaminants, by injecting them several miles underground, was tried up until the early 1970s with bizarre consequences. The deep injection well finally was abandoned because it was suspected of causing earthquakes in the Denver area.

The US Army, which owned the site, was willing to donate it—but not if there was going to be a community fight, Albin recalled. Yet a fight seemed unavoidable. Adams County, which long had felt it was being taken advantage of by Denver, was adamantly opposed to having expanded airport operations on the arsenal. "For years, Adams County felt it was a dumping ground," said Peña. "Very few positive assets were being built in Adams County." Instead, there were refineries and sewage treatment plants, even the Denver Union Stockyards, wafting their odors northward into the Adams County suburbs. Adams County officials weren't inclined to reward their big neighbor to the south by allowing it to build an airport in their midst.

The site selection study began in 1979 and took four years, reaching its conclusions as Denver was undergoing a mayoral election. All the candidates for mayor favored arsenal expansion. "No one had a problem with the arsenal. And then came Superfund," said James

"Skip" Spensley, the attorney charged with managing all of the studies and handling the diplomacy with local governments and local residents. Estimates of cleanup costs were in the billions of dollars. The daunting prospect forced arsenal backers to rethink their plans. Still, there were those who wondered what better way to use such a poisoned plot of land than to bury it under knee-deep concrete runways on a sprawling system of landing strips and taxiways where hardly any living soul would ever be exposed to the elements.

Albin remembers that he and Rex Jennings, then president of the Denver Metro Chamber, met with Sharon Proehl of the Metro North Chamber and Craig Carlson, a developer, "in a little hotel." They arrived at what they thought was a workable compromise: Denver would build a temporary east-west runway on the southern end of the arsenal, less affected by pollution, until a new airport could be put in place. But the Adams County commissioners didn't like that plan, either. That's when Denver's new mayor, Federico Peña, stepped in. "Peña just grabbed hold of it, sat down with the commissioners, and lo and behold, ended up signing that famous MOU… agreeing to just exactly that," Albin said.

In that memorandum of understanding (MOU), signed January 29, 1985, Denver addressed Adams County's concerns by agreeing not to build a new east-west runway on the southern tier of the arsenal site "if it is at all feasible" to transition to a new airport without it. For their part, the Adams County Commissioners agreed to support the election by which Denver would annex land for a new airport site and to amend their county land-use plan to recognize the emergence of an airport on land that had been dedicated to agriculture. When the new airport was completed—in any event, no later than 2000—Stapleton International Airport would shut down as an aviation facility.

Albin at first didn't think he and the new mayor would get along. "I thought, man, I'm not going to like this guy. He's this little liberal, Hispanic guy, all ambitious and everything. And I'm a kind of conservative guy. We sat down, and he said, 'Tell me what's happened so far.' And I did. He agreed that expansion on the Rocky Mountain Arsenal was probably the right solution, which is where I was at the time. And he jumped right in and took a real strong position and put the weight of the mayor's office behind it."

Peña often called on Albin, a self-described very liberal Democrat and very conservative Republican, to stand beside him at news conferences about the airport. If those two could agree, it would help convince others. "Look...we are absolutely bound in our determination that this is what the community needs." Albin said he and Peña became close friends. "And I'll tell you; Peña earned my undying respect during this whole thing. Because he turned out to be not only a visionary, but tough as nails and persistent as anybody I've ever seen in staying with the vision of a new airport and fighting every opponent who came along."

"Jobs, jobs, jobs"

An early 1987 study by Booz Allen Hamilton concluded a new airport would create 90,000 jobs. It would not only fix a problem, but it would be a huge generator of economic development. That was the big selling point, airport backers felt. But Skip Spensley felt that "all the talk of jobs, jobs, jobs belittled the real benefits of the airport." Yes, there would be plenty of work for people living in Adams County, but city civil service jobs, as required by city charter, would be held primarily by residents of Denver. The real benefits would be seen in the new developments around the airport, in the more efficient operation of air travel and, eventually, in the expansion of travel to international markets.

The Greater Denver Corporation's top agenda item was construction of DIA and the annexation election, said Tom Clark. The GDC put $700,000 on the table to win the election. At the time, Clark lived next door to a bricklayer named Bernie Montoya who kept asking him when the airport project finally would get underway. "These were my friends and my neighbors," Clark said. The recession was hitting them in the pocket, and they were eager to benefit from the economic stimulus the airport project would bring.

Union help was vital in the most highly unionized county in the state. Unions, realtors, developers—all got behind it. They contributed time, and those who could afford it contributed money. The bricklayers and pipefitters in particular knew they would benefit from the construction jobs, and there was a high concentration of union members in the building trades in Adams County. "If economic times had been better, annexation would have failed," Clark said. The airport "pumped a lot of money into that community." And Bernie Montoya was able to buy homes for all three of his kids, Clark said.

Because of the national administration's eagerness to increase air carrier capacity, Spensley was able to arrange an expedited environmental impact process, using an environmental assessment rather than the more complicated Environmental Impact Statement. It took about a year and a half off the usual five-year process, Spensley said. Still, the final assessment in April 1998 was two inches thick and weighed as much as a smallish cat.

There was no shortage of studies. In 1980, for example, an extensive Peat, Marwick, Mitchell & Co. study found a few Paleo-Indian sites that dated to 9000 BC on the prairie where the airport might go. There were, the consultants believed, sixty-two prehistoric and sixty-nine historic sites of some interest, but not much in the way of threatened plant or animal species. The area was "now mostly a botanical wasteland," the report said, and as for animals, "Prairie dogs are not considered a unique resource in the area."

That 1980 study called the arsenal expansion "questionable." The arsenal had the advantage of being closer to the densely populated core city, but perhaps it was too close to the mountains for bad-weather landings. There would be a loss of wildlife habitat, and 417 homes would have to be bought. Another Peat, Marwick, Mitchell & Co. study two years later also cited the potential overheating of tires as aircraft taxied out onto the far-flung arsenal runways. The study favored a site southwest of Bennett, between Box Elder and Kiowa creeks. Adding to the arguments for moving farther out were an estimated cost of up to $1 billion to make the arsenal land usable for an airport, and it would not be available until at least 2005. Also, Mayor Peña said in a 1989 memorandum, the arsenal wasn't big enough for the major airport Denver wanted, and "Denver and Adams County neighbors would suffer unacceptably high levels of noise and could stop any attempts to expand onto the Arsenal."

It was necessary for Denver to get the approval of Adams County voters because of another legacy of Colorado's populist political philosophy. In 1974, voters statewide approved a constitutional provision that applied only to annexations by the City and County of Denver. The Poundstone Amendment, named for suburban activist and lobbyist Freda Poundstone, required that all future annexations by the city had to be approved by a majority of the entire county in which the proposed annexation was to happen, not just in the specific area targeted to be annexed to Denver. The statewide ballot issue passed with a 61 percent majority at a time many suburban neighborhoods worried that being annexed by Denver would force their children to be bused to distant schools, because Denver was under federal court order to achieve better racial balance throughout its school district.

Since DIA was to be a city project, and not run by a regional airport authority or some other cooperative entity, the selling job was more difficult. There was some sentiment among Adams County officials for the county to strike out on its own, to build an Adams County International Airport. They'd own it and be able to put it where they wanted it. Adams County residents and homeowners in Montbello, which is part of Denver, opposed a Denver City Council condemnation ordinance that would have allowed an east-west runway to be built on the arsenal. Officials at the Buckley Air National Guard Base also opposed the new runway alignments, worried it would interfere with their military flight operations.

Much of this was happening with some comparatively new leadership in crucial positions. Denver mayor Federico Peña, governor Roy Romer, and Denver Metro Chamber CEO Dick Fleming all took office in 1983—Fleming, in fact, was hired the same week Romer was elected in 1982. Now, barely two years later, things were coming to a head. All of the candidates for Denver mayor in 1983 supported airport expansion onto the arsenal. Peña attended his first meeting of the DRCOG in late July 1983, three weeks after he took office. "I was brand-new," he said, and he quickly learned the intensity of Adams County's opposition to the arsenal plan. DRCOG members overall were 2 to 1 in favor of the arsenal expansion, "but everyone in Adams County was against it," Peña said. "They could block the project. They were already suing the city before I took office."

Peña, a lawyer, had been, as he put it, "sort of a neighborhood activist. I used to fight City Hall." He believed he knew how to reach out to the people in Adams County who felt they were being victimized by a government power play. He began meeting with Adams County officials, at first, he recalls, at a place called Bubba's Restaurant. "This kind of meeting had never happened before," he said.

But it was working. In late 1984, after a series of closed-door negotiations, Denver and Adams County officials jointly announced they were close to agreement on a new airport site, one that didn't involve the arsenal. On January 24, 1985, they made public their memorandum of understanding, reached after a year and a half of secret talks. Four days later, the MOU was officially signed.

Throughout the 1980s, the Denver Metro Chamber was playing an active role in airport planning. Responding in 1986 to a *Denver Post* columnist who had suggested the business community was not providing leadership on the issue, Richard Kirk, then chairman of the chamber's board, pointed out that the Denver Metro Chamber had been "represented at most, if not all" of the public hearings on the airport.

> In fact, it is generally well known that it was the Denver Chamber and MetroNorth Chamber that brought the governmental leaders of Denver and Adams County together several months ago to negotiate a compromise on the airport location. Leaders of the Denver Chamber of Commerce, including the Airport Task Force, and the Chamber's Board of Directors, have spent literally thousands of man-hours over the past six or eight years helping to bring the airport issue to where it is today.

It is not the chambers' style, Kirk wrote, "to wave placards or organize emotion-packed speeches to get their point across. It more often is our policy to study the issues, know the facts and let our position be known to the proper people, in the proper way, at the proper time."

Attorney Skip Spensley's job from the time he was hired in the mid-1980s was to facilitate dealing with the various levels of government, from Adams County, where the new airport was to be built, to the federal government, which required land-use studies and environmental impact assessments. "Four and a half years of politics" laid the foundation for the successful annexation vote in May 1988, Spensley said.

It was a difficult job, full of details, but it was to become even more difficult—and more of a diplomatic dilemma. Widespread serious opposition didn't really surface until the arsenal possibility was taken off the table. Older, deep-rooted residents resisted change, Albin said. They thought Stapleton was "just wonderful." They warned that an overly ambitious project could bankrupt the city. Taxes would go up, and it was impossible to change their minds. Denver may be overwhelmingly Democratic in voter registration, but that doesn't equate to the stereotypical liberal embrace of all things new and different.

Skip Spensely (left) with Mayor Peña. Photo courtesy of *The Denver Post*.

Albin said the most outspoken opponents included Denver advertising man Dick Chenoweth, the son of a former congressman; Dick Young, former chairman of the Denver Democrats and a rear admiral in the naval reserve; Adams County Commissioner Jim Nelms; aviation consultant Michael Boyd; "and of course Gene Amole," the very popular columnist for the *Rocky Mountain News*. "Amole represented that constituency," Albin said. "His scare tactic, which he knew to be wrong, was that it would bankrupt the city because our taxes would go up." In fact, the airport was to be constructed using federal ticket tax money and airport user fees, and Denver's new airport was at the top of the FAA's wish list, giving Denver priority access to an unused $6 billion in the Aviation Trust Fund.

Albin invited Amole on a tour of the site, hoping to sway him. He booked eleven different experts to pitch the airport to the columnist. "He was the only audience...We were there for hours." But it didn't change Amole's mind. The next day his column appeared in the *Rocky Mountain News* with the headline "Thanks, but no thanks." "He went right into the same rant," Albin said. These weren't general obligation bonds; they were revenue bonds. Those who used the airport would pay for it. But Albin said Amole "refused to acknowledge that fact."

The Chamber's Role

For ten years, Spensley said, the Denver Metro Chamber was a major advocate of building on the arsenal. "But they were smart enough to say...'You're the experts.'" It would have been a mistake to find a solution that fit the politics of the situation. The trick was to "find the answer and then consider the politics," Spensley said. Adams County threatened a lawsuit—at one point, Dick Fleming remembers the county's attorney, Eliot Cutler, threatening to "sue you until hell freezes over" if the airport were expanded onto the arsenal—but Spensley said as negotiations proceeded, Adams County really wanted to find a solution. A lawsuit would have been a comparatively quick way to stall or stop the construction project, but by now Cutler was "very collaborative" in his approach, Spensley said, as were city representatives Tom Gougeon of Denver and Aurora mayor Paul Tauer. On the various parties' wish lists, Spensley said, "85 percent of the items were identical."

Spensley worked constantly to anticipate problems and address them. He had to find out whether there were enough labor and cement available to tackle a project of this size. He had to deal with angry residents at Eastwood Estates, whose homes were in the path of airport expansion no matter where it went. His diplomacy was so successful that one year, he said, he "was invited to Thanksgiving dinner with the Eastwood Estates folks." One of his more delicate challenges was dealing with Native Americans who had raised the argument that the airport construction would disturb ancient Indian burial sites. After meeting for three hours at a motel on East Colfax Avenue, a plan was agreed on. A bus was hired to take representatives of the Native Americans out to the airport site to perform a blessing ceremony. Spensley said the octogenarian shaman of the group told him it was the first time a white person had asked him to bless a site like that. "That shows how important it is to involve everyone," Spensley said.

Denver, 1941

Rooftop view of Seventeenth Street in downtown Denver. Photo courtesy of the Denver Public Library Western History Collection, X-23048.

Chapter 8

Winning Two Elections

The Denver area's business community has been involved in a lot of efforts over the past century and a half to assure the health of the region's economy, to keep up the energy level, and to inject new life when things seemed to be flagging. But "the biggest shining star of all of these has been DIA," said M. Doak Jacoway, president of Jacoway Financial Corp., a Denver-based estate and investment advising firm.

Jacoway, who was chairman of the Denver Metro Chamber in 2001-02, points out that the chamber was involved in every one of the major infrastructure projects of the 1990s. But nothing was more important, he said, and nothing preoccupied the chamber more, than building a new airport.

Jacoway is not a big-spending, big-government type. He's a conservative Republican. But sometimes it takes a major government investment to bring the economy back to life, and that kind of investment can't succeed without support from the business community. The role of business, Jacoway said, is to serve as a sounding board for the viability of the idea, and then to raise the money and provide a lot of the foot soldiers for the inevitable campaign. In Colorado, those campaigns are a fact of life because of the state's unique requirement that voters approve any new tax—a requirement that has created a culture that voters really ought to have a say on any major new investment of public funds.

The Denver Metro Chamber, as a whole, is "not dying to impose new taxes," said political consultant and pollster Floyd Ciruli. But "there has been a major change in the chamber's outlook" over the past couple of decades. It has become "a very progressive, anti-TABOR" chamber, Ciruli said. "It is just so totally different it's unbelievable."

TABOR is the constitutional requirement, imposed after voters approved it in the 1992 election, that said any increase in government revenue that exceeds the rate of inflation must either be approved by voters or returned to taxpayers. The first several years it was in effect, there were no refunds, because the economy was still recovering from the down years of the late '80s. The amendment, which passed as a ballot issue, also requires a vote on any proposed tax increase. And there's another state constitutional amendment that requires everyone in any county affected by a proposed Denver annexation to approve the transfer of jurisdiction. So there was no way, legally or politically, that an airport could have been attempted without first winning public support. Adams County voters and then, a year later, Denver voters had to be convinced that DIA was in their best interests.

"The new airport couldn't have been built if it hadn't been for the economic downturn of the late 1980s," said John Frew, the mastermind behind the campaign strategies and most of the tactical details, too. It was a complicated management challenge, Frew said, like the carnival game Whac-A-Mole—new problems just kept cropping up. "To answer one question you had to answer ten others," Frew recalled.

Attorney Skip Spensley was brought on board in the mid-1980s to run what became the New Airport Office, which meant dealing with both the bureaucracy and the politics of the massive project. In addition to shepherding the airport project through the maze of

John Frew, 1988. Photo courtesy of the Denver Public Library Western History Collection.

environmental, safety, transportation, and other regulations, Spensley had an election to worry about. "I don't like politics," Spensley said. "I like policy makers, I like the political process, but I don't like politics." Nonetheless, he became heavily involved with both.

Spensley, with an extensive background in environmental law, also had to be a diplomat. In addition to expediting the government permitting process, the lanky, plainspoken attorney also was required to use his charm to win over voters—especially those in the Adams County and northeast Denver communities that would be most directly impacted by the new airport's need for land and its eventual operational inconveniences, including a much longer driving distance and a new noise footprint. Spensley averaged three public meetings a week for five years, enduring a "brutal commute" back and forth from his home in Boulder.

At any point, a lawsuit could have stopped the process, he said. Opponents of the project in Aurora and Adams County threatened to go to court, but Spensley believes they really wanted to find a mutually acceptable solution. Aurora and Adams County had hired Washington, DC, attorney Eliot Cutler to represent their interests. Cutler had a reputation for knowing how to use environmental laws to stop airports from expanding. But Spensley said it turned out to be more of a collaborative than confrontational series of negotiations. "We would never have been able to go to an annexation election without Adams County going along," he pointed out. Some Adams County officials thought Cutler was maybe just a bit too collaborative. Former county commissioner Jim Nelms told the *St. Louis Business Journal* in 1996 that "the only thing he [Cutler] did for Adams County is get them to give away 53 square miles of land to the City of Denver."

Early Public Involvement

The business community's role "was a partnership of a lot of different interests. I don't think anybody deserves more credit than others," Spensley said. He mentioned a few individuals in particular, though—Bob Albin, Dick Fleming, Len Perlmutter, Gail Klapper, former chair—saying "all played a role telling people it had economic benefits for them." Labor unions pitched in too, as did the entrepreneurial community, by raising money and providing volunteers. "There wasn't a role for them to play until we got to the campaign," Spensley said, but once the campaign started, it was important to get the public involved early. And there was ample help. "It was as much a political process as a technical process."

First, Adams County had to be convinced. Mayor Peña couldn't be seen as the face of the campaign. But Governor Romer showed up regularly in opinion polls as perhaps the most popular politician in the state. Even though, as Peña pointed out, "the state has very little role" in the airport project, it would have been politically risky for the Denver mayor to take a very large role in promoting Denver's annexation of Adams County land. "I was being perceived as a Denver-centric mayor," Peña said. "It would have been difficult for me to go to Adams County and say, 'This is good for you.'" Romer and Peña both put their personal ambitions aside to get the airport approved by the voters, Bob Albin said.

Peña knew he was not popular in Adams County, but Romer didn't have that problem. The governor campaigned for the new airport at dozens of cafes and coffee shops around Adams County. He stayed out of Peña's way, Albin said, and "there was no jealousy on Peña's part even though he'd been working on it [the airport project] for years."

Romer remembers it as "a very tough sell…We were taking Adams County land and leaving them with noise." But building the airport, he said, was "very much a part of my agenda." It meant jobs, and that's what Colorado needed. "I knew it was going to take extra effort. I decided to make it personal." So for three months, at 5:30, 6:30, and 7:30 in the morning, Romer would put on his weathered leather jacket, head to a cafe or diner somewhere in Adams County and have breakfast. It was always the same thing: oatmeal. No sugar, no milk, just oatmeal. "I mapped out every restaurant in Adams County," he said, and even ran through the list completely and started revisiting places. It got so he didn't even need to order; the proprietor had a bowl of oatmeal waiting for him when he sat down.

He recalls walking into one place at 5:30 in the morning where one of the other customers told him, "C'mon. You're not the governor; I've seen you down at the mission." There was the chicken farmer in Fort Lupton who wanted the government to soundproof her barn if jets were going to be roaring about overhead. "We ended up buying that place," Romer said. After three months of this, gulping down a few spoonfuls of bland oatmeal at every stop, "My cholesterol level went down," the former governor said. "My doctor told me, 'My God, Romer, you've got the cholesterol of a 16-year-old girl.'" It was good for his mental health as well as his physical health, he recalls. "It was joyous...One of the most satisfying outreaches I made as governor."

"Don't underestimate the impact he [Romer] had," Albin said. "You have to give him tremendous credit...Romer was willing and Peña was smart enough to ask him to step in and spend his political capital...and Peña never showed the slightest bit of jealousy that Romer was getting the credit." Both of them "put their personal ambitions aside to do what was best for the state," Albin said.

Frew handled the Adams County campaign and "was a genius at it," Albin said. Adams County commissioner Steve Cramer was chairman of Adams County Partners in Progress for a New Airport, and Frew was the campaign director. Spensley was the lead consultant. "And then we had a bunch of business people like me who were giving speeches and talking to city councils," Albin said.

Walt Imhoff, CEO of investment bankers Hanifen, Imhoff Inc., wrote a letter to Bruce Rockwell of the chamber's airport finance and development strategy group that offers an example of the business community's participation. The letter, dated September 20, 1989, reads: "During the two airport elections, our firm was responsible for raising approximately $140,000 in contributions, contributed the time of not less than fifty of our employees to telethons, get-out-the-vote efforts, and toured the city prior to the election to promote the airport to the electorate."

Some critics have said that metro area counties other than Denver and Adams weren't involved in the negotiations, even though they had a heavy investment in the outcome. It's not true, Frew said. "Oh, they were involved." Elected officials from all over the metro area were regularly negotiating with one another. The airport is where it is because everyone was talking and eventually reached agreement, Frew said. It would not have happened without bringing the other metropolitan area counties on board, and that required a bipartisan political network as well as a commitment from the private sector. "It was just the most amazing volunteer network," Frew said. "The business community was galvanized...We asked for 100 volunteers and got 150."

Tom Clark said Frew told him the strategy was to "win this election one voter at a time." The group working on the campaign was using computers, a tool comparatively new to politics, to target specific blocks that needed to be worked. Computers have come a long way since the late-1980s models the campaign was using. The computers weren't very fast, but they were effective. "Frew ran really an incredible campaign," Clark said. It was door-to-door, and union help was "vital" in the most highly unionized county in the state—especially bringing aboard pipefitters and bricklayers like Clark's job-hungry neighbor Bernie Montoya. If the region's economy had been better, annexation would have failed, Clark believes. The pressing issue was jobs—immediately, in building the airport, and long-range, at the concessions and airline ticket counters and baggage operations.

To much of Adams County, Clark said, "It sure looked like a Denver takeover," with big business working with "a bigger-than-life CEO in Dick Fleming." Adams County Commissioner Cramer, a real visionary in Clark's assessment, "was taking a huge amount of grief" because of his support of the project. Steve Cramer was chairman of the pro-airport Adams County Partners in Progress for a New Airport. His fellow Adams County Republicans challenged him, and he lost a bid for re-election. "He is the unsung hero of the airport," Clark said.

Frew was doing almost daily polling, and the polls were showing a very tight race. Then, just four days before the election, the numbers plummeted. The survey results came out on Friday. Frew, without telling anyone else, spent $100,000 on advertising that weekend. When the annexation won by 8 percentage points, Don Bain told other members of the chamber, as Clark remembers it, "I thought we were buying an election; I didn't know we were buying a landslide." (Bain doesn't remember saying it, but he said he's happy to take credit for it.)

Buying and Selling Land

With the prospect of a multibillion dollar project being built in their midst, the people who owned land in the airport area were busily trading. There is always suspicion about large contributions from people who would profit in a big way from the election; it wouldn't help to add the landowners to that political mix.

Critics of the project already were complaining that the new airport was unnecessary, too far away, too expensive, and too lucrative for just a few people. Big projects, they warned, mean big potential for graft and corruption. The conservative-leaning *National Journal* wrote critically of the airport project that the chairman of the appropriations subcommittee on transportation, Senator Frank Lautenberg, Democrat from New Jersey, raised $100,000 from supporters in Colorado—not exactly in his district. The *National Journal* speculated that the FAA was not as skeptical as it might have been about DIA because its officials were anxious to pad their résumés with their roles in launching the most ambitious airport project in years.

The Denver Post reported in December 1990 that DIA was the focus of speculative real estate deals by savings and loans and developers, adding $24 million, the *Post* said, to what taxpayers were paying for the property. Michael Boyd, the airline consultant who was one of the project's harshest critics, called it "a major scandal" in testimony on May 2, 1991, before the House Appropriations Subcommittee on Transportation. "It approaches the depth and proportions of the savings and loan morass," Boyd said.

And yet the evidence strongly suggests that DIA was about as clean as a project of that size could be. It was accomplished with "a minimal amount of corruption and graft and cronyism," Albin said. "You'll probably hear someplace along the way that the airport is located where it is because Peña was paid off by developers to put it on their property...That is a total fabrication. That site was chosen in general...by that group that met up in Adams County. Secondly, there wasn't any other place it could go."

Some critics cannot be convinced that some sort of graft or impropriety was not involved in the trading of land at and surrounding the new airport site. At the very least, landowners who benefited from the decision may have influenced the planning, the critics feel. The unease persists despite the findings of a 1991 investigation by the Colorado Attorney General's Office into "whether any property owners or others used, or attempted to use, illegal methods to influence City or County officials in this process" of site selection. The attorney general concluded that "the investigation has not uncovered any evidence that any City or County officials were illegally influenced in their decisions concerning the selection of airport sites."

The process "was mostly what was to be expected," said real estate expert Peter Bowes. His Bowes and Company, a Denver-based appraisal and counseling firm, was involved in one court case involving the condemnation of 20,000 acres of airport land. The acquisition of land for the new airport was, he and other appraisers testified, a clean process, and in

Bowes' opinion, Denver got "astonishing" value for the airport land.

"People say [projects like the airport] happen only because people are enriching themselves," said Skip Spensley. "I never saw that." Three University of Denver authors of a 1997 book about the airport ("I used to teach with them," Spensley noted) were among the critics who "took a jaundiced view of how everybody was lining their pockets. And, really, there was nothing going on," Spensley said. "We got a bargain deal."

Former Denver mayor Bill McNichols and former Colorado attorney general J. D. MacFarlane were among the skeptics. McNichols and another former Denver mayor, Tom Currigan, also explained their concerns in congressional testimony. On the other side were supporters like Bill Daniels, the cable television pioneer, who in February 1989 threatened to move his headquarters from Denver if the airport wasn't built. He also said it was time the region improved its economic development efforts and its image. "Denver has been sending a message to the rest of the world, and that message is, 'We don't want you,'" Daniels said.

Michael Boyd acknowledges that he got a national reputation thanks to the airport and the attention his critiques of the project and the campaign got in the press. "The data they were using was just all bogus," he said of the airport's supporters. "The process was dishonest and untrue…I maintain we'd be better off today if we'd kept Stapleton. Of course, $5 billion is a lot of economic impact."

Roger Ailes ran the opposition campaign, funded largely by hotels operating at the soon-to-be-closed Stapleton. Originally called Save Our Stapleton, the campaign slogan became a more direct Let's Vote No. The proponents, not surprisingly, were calling their campaign Let's Vote Yes! The pro side's steering committee had forty-two members. Supporters of the new airport made Ailes an issue, too. With his reputation for negative political campaigning, he was easily as much of a liability as an asset for the airport opponents.

Adams County Said "Yes"

On May 17, 1988, Adams County voters approved annexation by an 8 percentage point margin, 54 to 46 percent. But opponents of the project, especially Dick Young and Bill Chenoweth, insisted that Denver voters have a say, too. They threatened to start a petition drive to force an election. At a January 1989 meeting of airport supporters sponsored by several chambers of commerce, former

Roy Romer at the 1988 Adams County Annexation Election. Photo courtesy of the Denver Public Library Western History Collection.

governor Roy Romer vowed to "roll over and crush" the opposition. He got a big hand at the time but later conceded that it was probably not the most diplomatic thing to say.

Somewhat exasperated, but nonetheless confident, Mayor Peña decided not to try to stall or get involved in a protracted debate and instead called for a vote. City Council agreed with him. Peña turned the tables on the opposition, said John Frew, the airport campaign manager. He said the mayor told him, "Let's run right at them; let's put it on the ballot ourselves."

Airport supporters say one of the turning points in the Denver campaign was when Young and Chenoweth declined to appear for a debate, citing their disagreements with the sponsoring Denver Metro Chamber of Commerce and its tactics. Instead, they were represented on the dais by two empty chairs. Roger Ogden, then chairman of the chamber, accused the opponents of "diversionary tactics." Denver was voting on whether to build an airport, he wrote in a March 31 note to Young and Chenoweth, "not on whether they agree with your assessment of the Greater Denver Corporation and the Chamber of Commerce." Frew, in a post-election note to Bob Albin, wrote, "I'll always remember the chamber 'empty chair' debate as the beginning of the end for Young & Chenoweth."

On May 16, 1989, Denverites gave almost 2 to 1 support to the new airport. With a 41 percent turnout of registered voters, 63 percent were in favor and only 37 percent opposed. "What you heard from the voters was the sound of Denver taking off," Peña said at an exuberant election-night party. "This is a victory of optimism over pessimism that will be heard all around the world."

Urban affairs columnist Neal Peirce, in a May 26, 1989, speech at the annual meeting of the Greater Denver Chamber of Commerce, congratulated Denver voters and the successful campaign to get their approval. "Let me say I was impressed by the professionalism by which the 'yes' campaign was conducted," Peirce said. "Obviously my old friend Dick Fleming, whom I regard as one of the country's greatest civic entrepreneurs, had a lot to do with it. But clearly he was just one player. For it was not just the bundle of money a lot of you in the room had to throw in—and I understand it was quite a bundle. But the clear, direct, pointed campaign materials. The outreach and coalition building. Coming on top of your victory in the Adams County vote last year, you Denverites seem to be gaining a talent for taking things to the polls, to the people, that the civic leaderships in some other towns might envy."

Mayor Peña quickly put the airport on a fast-track construction schedule, aiming at a 1992 completion date. It was going to be the first airport constructed in the United States since the Dallas–Fort Worth mega-airport was completed in 1974. And, as has been evident since, DIA may turn out to be the last entirely new US airport. The hurdles Denver faced—the bureaucracy, the economy, the environmental concerns—are still there and in some cases are more problematic.

Time magazine reflected the generally accepted interpretation that the Denver election was a vote to get the city's economy rolling again. On the same day, *Time* pointed out, in Seattle, "the spirit of Western boosterism took a fall almost as jarring as the Denver vote was exhilarating." Seattle voters, with a turnout half the size of Denver's but a similar proportion of approval, imposed strict size-and-height restrictions on new downtown buildings. "Had the two cities traded economies, the results might have been reversed," *Time* speculated. Seattle was booming, and building—maybe too fast to suit some residents. "Denver, once riding high on an energy boom, has been slumping for the past four years," *Time* said. "In that climate, voters bought the promises of Romer and Peña that a new airport would mean jobs and prosperity."

The climate of that time is reflected in the conclusion to *Time's* May 29, 1989, article: "It is only in the nation's booming Seattles, it seems, that residents can ask, What price growth? In the depressed Denvers, even the hope of growth seems to be worth almost any price."

Denver, May 3, 1950

View of Sixteenth Street at dawn. Photo courtesy of the Denver Public Library Western History Collection, Bill Peery, X23377.

Chapter 9

Buyer's Remorse

In their 1997 book, *Denver International Airport: Lessons Learned,* three scholars from the University of Denver refer to a February 1995 *Rocky Mountain News* article that quoted what the *News* writer described as "the touching *mea culpa* of a former editor." This former editor of the *News* was talking about the Denver news media's failure to be sufficiently skeptical about the airport project early on. "It was a mistake," he said. "I know that now. I just bleed for the city. I think it's just tragic. I was wrong and so were most of the other people who had anything to do with it...This thing—it's just horrible."

Almost no one still holds such an apocalyptic or melodramatic view of the decision to build DIA. The authors of that 1997 book—Paul Stephen Dempsey, Andrew R. Goetz, and Joseph S. Szyliowicz—acknowledge that the new airport's fans today far outnumber its die-hard critics. But for months, even years, after the new airport opened, it appeared the critics were right. Continental had abandoned Denver as a hub. Because airlines were paying higher airport fees, the fares they passed on to Denver customers were higher than elsewhere in the country. The fancy new high-tech baggage system

A gargoyle sculpture contemplates the baggage system woes at Denver International Airport soon after the airport's opening. Photo © 2011 Barbara Norton.

A rendering of the plan for Denver International Airport. Photo courtesy of the Denver Public Library Western History Collection.

never would work right. Some Denverites were traveling an hour or more to the south end of Colorado Springs to take cheaper flights from the Colorado Springs Airport.

On the day the airport opened, February 28, 1995, the Boulder polling firm Talmey-Drake Research & Strategy, Inc. released a survey that showed how people had soured on the project. The poll showed that only 33 percent now favored building the airport compared with 63 percent who were opposed. The Denver vote in 1989 had been almost the reverse: 63 to 37 percent in favor of proceeding.

Newsweek's June 7, 1993, issue called the airport "civic boosterism run wild." *The Wall Street Journal* called it a "disaster" and picked up the taunting name "Peña's Folly." The former mayor was by then the US secretary of transportation, having been appointed by the newly elected president Bill Clinton. *National Journal* criticized the political deals that cleared the way for the new airport, though the major "deal" appeared to be the rather open settlement of a lawsuit brought by the noise-impacted Park Hill neighborhood. The settlement stipulated that Stapleton would be closed to any airplane traffic once the new airport was operational.

The fit of rue continued for close to two years after the airport opened. The airport project had been inexcusably delayed, the critics said. It had generated a great deal of negative publicity nationally. Negotiations with Continental and United Airlines stalled over rent. "It's somewhat grand and could make Denver uncompetitive with other hubs like Dallas and Salt Lake City," United's Ed Nielson told *The New*

Constructing the main terminal at Denver International Airport. Photo courtesy of the Denver Public Library Western History Collection.

York Times. And, for all the complaining about how far the airport was from any populated area, there were those who had even other ideas. In that same July 31, 1988, *Times* article, Reuben Espinosa, founder of a citizens' group called Committee for a Better Airport, said, "We're not opposed to a new airport. We're opposed to the new airport site. We think it should be 10 miles farther east."

There was no shortage of airport-related problems during the construction process. Continental Airlines, one of the three carriers using Denver as a hub, filed for Chapter 11 bankruptcy in late 1990. US Representative Frank Wolf, Republican from Virginia, tried to stop DIA construction because Denver was bidding against his district to build an auxiliary of the Smithsonian's air and space museum (Virginia won). Airport bonds were put on a "credit watch" by Wall Street. A terminal design proposed by the Perez Group of New Orleans was criticized by aviation manager George Doughty as "commonplace and indistinctive." The airport design committee didn't like it either, and Perez was replaced by Denver-based C. W. Fentress, J. H. Bradburn and Associates, designers of the landmark roof. United and Continental airlines dragged their feet, saying a new airport could wait another decade, until 1998. World Port at Denver International Airport, an attempt to create "an international air cargo hub" at the new airport, didn't achieve its lofty goals, due in part to the presence of nearby Front Range Airport, which had its own dreams of air-cargo dominance. Continental tried, but failed, to get the Park Hill neighborhood's permission for an exception to the agreement that Stapleton would no longer be used for any aviation operations; it wanted to continue to base its maintenance facility there. Albin notes that Continental, which by then had a new president, Frank Lorenzo, had won the prime Concourse A location "and then essentially pulled out."

There were key personnel changes, too. "In one year we lost the three top people involved in the airport," former mayor Wellington Webb said. Bill Smith, the director of public works and then in charge of airport operations, died of a brain tumor. Ginger Evans, who was running Stapleton, left soon after Smith's death. George Doughty, the city's aviation director, also quit in 1992 to run a small regional airport near Allentown, Pennsylvania. Albin said Doughty left because he disapproved of the way Webb was supervising the project. He said Doughty told him, "Somebody's going to take a fall for this, and I'm not going to be the guy."

Familiar Complaints

Former mayor Federico Peña observed that a lot of the same criticisms made about DIA were made of the decision to build Stapleton more than sixty years earlier—"almost verbatim." Stapleton's "Folly" even was criticized for being too far out on the prairie, when eventually the problem was that it was too close for comfort. Similarly, the early criticisms of DIA have proven to be exaggerated, Peña said. Critics said DIA would never make money. "It never lost a dime," the former mayor said. They said it was too expensive. "At the beginning," Peña concedes. But even then, airlines were struggling to pay for fuel. "Their costs are not driven by landing fees." And the people who bought airport bonds, he pointed out, "did very well."

In a 1995 interview, Jim DeLong, then the city's airport director, said that while Peña is remembered for his vision in imagining a great airport, it was Webb who had to complete the project. "It is significantly more difficult and less glamorous to complete a megaproject than it is to begin it," DeLong told Paul Dempsey and the other authors of the 1997 book critiquing the DIA process.

Now most of the critics have changed their tune. Former mayor Wellington Webb said even the late Gene Amole, the *Rocky Mountain News* columnist who was an implacable airport critic, eventually admitted to him that it was a good airport, but that "it ought to be, for the amount of money it cost."

"I think the public has swung," said Joseph Szyliowicz, another of the authors of the 1997 book. "People today have come to value the airport." There's a psychological phenomenon involved, said Szyliowicz. People become attached to the things they may at one time have thought they spent too much money to get. "They tend to get...a warm, fuzzy glow...The more you spend, the more you love it."

Dempsey also finds much to praise in the new facility. "DIA has been a tremendous success in providing enormous capacity for growth over a long time horizon," he wrote. But problems remain. "The city's altitude will continue to be a challenge for intercontinental traffic, but its geography works well as a North American connecting hub."

And Dempsey still blames mismanagement by the Webb administration for driving up the costs of the airport "radically and unnecessarily." Taxpayers may not have been left holding the bag, but travelers using the airport had to pay more. "Fortunately, traffic growth eventually was able to absorb those costs," Dempsey said. Both he and Szyliowicz lament the delay in getting some sort of rail system to serve the airport; the airport's distance from population centers makes motor vehicle pollution a serious issue. Mass transit of some sort "should be a top priority," Szyliowicz said. Dempsey also criticized "the reliance on cutting-edge technology in the baggage and people-mover systems without adequate back-up systems in place."

There's no bigger airport booster than Albin, but he has similar complaints. They mostly have to do with the Webb administration. "I obviously thought Webb was a very poor administrator," he said, ticking off the ways in which he thinks the DIA project could have been better: Webb disbanded Peña's airport design committee in August 1991 and went along with an unproven automated baggage system that the committee wanted to scrap; instead, the baggage-battering system became the butt of late-night TV comedy. Car rental agencies lobbied successfully to put their operations off-site instead of in the lower floors of the parking garages, where the original plan called for them to go. An airport hotel was supposed to be ready for the opening but years later was still in the planning stages. Peña Boulevard could have been made six lanes wide instead of four while everyone was waiting for the baggage system to be done. And, Albin said, Front Range Airport could have been bought comparatively inexpensively to avoid potential competition and operating conflicts with DIA. But none of it happened. The airport "is not what it could have been," Albin said. And he blames Webb.

"Those are the things that happened with the Webb administration that didn't really get coverage," Albin said. "And, more power to Webb, he got the airport built, he got it open, and it's a huge success. But it is not what it could have been."

The baggage system, Tom Clark said, "was a big black eye...Jay Leno material." Webb was known for getting things done, but his personal style "was just very suspicious, abrasive," Clark said. Webb was confrontational with the airlines; Clark said the mayor's only friend in Adams County was Thornton Mayor Margaret Carpenter. And yet, despite the added costs and that notorious baggage system, "the real nuts and bolts of putting it together were a credit to Webb,"

Clark said. And, on opening day, three aircraft were able to land simultaneously in a snowstorm—validating a major reason for undertaking such a vast project.

Webb In for Peña

Webb was the surprise winner of the 1991 mayoral race. Peña had announced the previous November that he would not run for a third term. The smart money was on Norm Early, Denver's dapper district attorney, whose easygoing style contrasted with Webb's sometimes brusque demeanor. Don Bain, the only Republican in the race, had an uphill fight, given Denver's heavily Democratic voter registration. (Municipal elections are by law nonpartisan, but most everybody knows who is registered with what party.) But Bain did have a certain appeal to a large segment of the city's old guard, because he wanted to delay construction on the increasingly expensive and complicated airport project. Although he was a supporter of the annexation and Denver airport votes, Bain in 1991 wanted to put construction on hold for two years, put bond sales on hold, and replace the airport management team.

Real estate appraiser Peter Bowes has some minor criticisms of the actual construction of the airport. There should have been a rail station for mass-transit access to the terminal, for example, and there should be better walkways for when the underground trains break down. But he said he couldn't back Bain in the 1991 Denver mayoral election because of Bain's position that construction on the airport should have been put on hold. "That did it for me," Bowes said. He ended up supporting Webb because he admired his energy.

Denver mayor Wellington Webb. Photo courtesy of the Denver Public Library Western History Collection, Wilken Photography #2.

"I think that's one reason people elected me in '91," Webb said. Bain was against the airport, and Early was "a real cheerleader." Webb represented a middle ground. "I was a cheerleader with reservations about how difficult this project would be."

Webb also walked the city. Door-to-door, face-to-face contact was part of his winning strategy. His battered sneakers from that campaign are buried in a time capsule at DIA. Outspent more than 3 to 1, Webb nonetheless won a runoff election against Early with 58 percent of the vote. In a city with a comparatively small African American population, it's remarkable that the two runoff contenders were both black. But then, Denver had just elected a Hispanic mayor to two consecutive terms.

That evidence of a sweet new world of post-racial inclusiveness needs to be put in perspective, though. Both mayors had to endure a lot of criticism, and some of that criticism likely had a racial element. Peña was Denver's first Hispanic mayor; Webb the first African American. People were used to a little cronyism in high municipal office, but these new cronies didn't have pink faces; they came in various shades of brown. It would be a mistake to dismiss such concerns as unfounded; after all, sixty years earlier the city and state governments were briefly controlled by the Ku Klux Klan. But it's a worse mistake to overstate their impact. If there was backlash—and there was—it was most likely due more to a resistance to change than to any ingrained stereotype. Things were moving too fast to suit some; the ambition of the new politicians was unseemly somehow, even if ambition of any stripe or color is not at all unusual in the world of politics. Frew, the airport campaign manager, said having the first Hispanic mayor "was unsettling to a lot of people." There was even a recall effort—which ultimately failed because the recall proponents couldn't get enough signatures. "Then it became, 'Let's stop his favorite project,'" Frew said. The mayor's political opponents shifted their attention to the airport.

When ground finally was broken for the airport project in 1989, "The economy was in the pits," Webb said. The project brought in ten thousand construction workers. "A variety of contractors, big as well as small…not only did it fix the aviation problem, it also put people back to work," Webb said. "The airport did what it was supposed to do." It stimulated growth in the northern part of Denver and the southern part of Adams County. Growth continues around the airport site, following the example of development trends around Dulles International Airport outside Washington, DC, or the Dallas–Fort Worth airport complex. What were once fairly isolated sites have become cores for shipping, warehousing, lodging, and other businesses that prefer being close to transportation.

And yet, not long after the new airport opened, the once-supportive press began to question the airport project, and Webb's management of it. But Webb said he doesn't remember much about that. "Our press was so bad at that point I didn't read it." He did make a promise, though: "If I can't get it open, I won't run for reelection."

Webb appreciates the support he got from the business community. "During my tenure was probably the greatest building boom in Denver history," he said. "The business community was certainly a great cheerleader for most of the economic development projects that we had." Business leaders were "very supportive of my administration in many of the bond issues that were passed."

There's no denying, though, that the airport was a problem. "We had to redesign 85 percent of the airport," he said, and the automated baggage system that United Airlines wanted "was a significant change order." The baggage system also was largely responsible, especially in the later stages of construction, for an embarrassing series of postponements and delays. And the delays raised the price, from estimates as low as $1.7 billion in the beginning to the final overall cost of close to $5 billion.

The new airport's opening date, originally set by Mayor Peña for sometime in 1992, was changed half a dozen times after regional voters gave their go-ahead for the project. October 1993 became the operating target date. That was then clarified to October 29. A gala fundraiser was planned for the following month, November 1993, for the purpose of "creating an evening exciting and fulfilling for Coloradans to learn about [DIA] and celebrate its successful conclusion." Nearly four thousand guests raised $578,000 for United Way and toasted the honored guest, Federico Peña, who was by then secretary of transportation. The airport hadn't opened, though; the opening date had been postponed to December 19, 1993. Then it became March 9, 1994; and finally, two weeks before the latest opening date of May 15, 1994, Webb announced he wasn't going to make any more announcements. The airport finally opened on February 28, 1995.

Interior of DIA's terminal. Photo © 2011 Willie Gibson.

Webb said a lot of people thought the airport should have been built between Denver and Colorado Springs. But land costs there were prohibitive, and the hilly, rocky terrain—including the Palmer Divide, often a driving hazard in snow—was not as suitable for an airport. Still, after the airport opened, many airline customers from Denver chose to fly out of Colorado Springs, because airfares were less expensive there.

The new airport didn't stop the complaints about noise, either. They no longer came from Park Hill, but from suburbs more distant from the core city. And many of the complaints were filed by the same people. The first 58,000 noise complaints were filed from 3,000 individual households—an average of almost 20 per family. In fact, 10 families accounted for fully a quarter of the complaints, and one family alone was responsible for almost 6,000 complaints, or 11 percent of the total.

Paul Dempsey was also on the board of the new, restructured Frontier Airlines when he testified before a congressional subcommittee on March 5, 1998. He was highly critical of United Airlines' attempt to dominate the regional market. He told the transportation subcommittee of the Senate Appropriations Committee that United "has been on a relentless 15-year homicidal mission to destroy competition and create a fortress hub monopoly at Denver." He said United also went after Western Pacific, a new carrier using Colorado Springs as a hub. He recalled how United tried to get Ginger Evans, then DIA's chief engineer, to paint over the windows on the pedestrian bridge to Concourse A, used by competing airlines. She refused to ruin the view, however. United, the only major airline to support deregulation in the 1970s, originally did not want to go to DIA, Dempsey said, nor would it work with the city on an alternative to its favored automated baggage system. United wanted to dominate the Denver commercial air traffic market, Dempsey said, because it "is estimated to be about a $5 billion revenue prize."

Michael Boyd also testified to that same subcommittee on the same day, saying it would be a mistake to build new airports following the DIA model. "We need airport capacity," Boyd said, "but we need it built where it is necessary, not just new airports that cost too much for airlines to fly to." He mentioned DIA and an airport in West Virginia as examples. He also took more than a little pride in his notoriety for being "a contrarian," as he phrased it. "I have a reputation (of which I am proud, by the way) of being often blunt and to the point."

Boyd still believes the airport was sold to the voters under false pretenses. "It was built on lies and doctored data," he said. "I stand on that." He maintains that Denver could have saved a lot of money if it had kept Stapleton as an operating airport. "We would have had growth anyway. [DIA] hasn't attracted new airlines…We lost one whole connecting hub."

And yet he has softened his position—a little. "The way [the airport] has been run over the past ten years, it's worth supporting…Can we be happy it's here? Yeah. Can we be proud of the process that got it here? I don't think so."

Problems Addressed

Clark remembers that critics would ask him, shortly after DIA opened, "If you're such a hot airport, why isn't Southwest [Airlines] there?" Because, Clark said, Southwest president Herb Kelleher "had some personal issue with Peña," who had by then moved on to the job of secretary of transportation—and who, by the way, is a fan of Southwest.

The day Kelleher left as Southwest's president "is the day Southwest came to see us," Clark said. The low-cost carrier is now DIA's third-largest in terms of passenger usage, and the so-called "Southwest Effect" has worked to lower airfares across the board. Thanks to fare battles among United, Frontier, and Southwest, DIA flyers pay less than they did right after the airport opened.

Nationally, about 900 million passengers a year use US airports, according to the FAA. About 50 million of them fly through DIA, and the numbers continue to increase. Because of Denver's isolation from other major population centers, it reverses the usual airport ratio of passengers changing planes to those beginning or ending their travels in Denver. At DIA, 40 percent of the passengers are transferring; 60 percent are what is known in the aviation industry as "O&D"—origin and destination—passengers.

At 16,000 feet, DIA's longest runway, the longest commercial aviation runway in North America, makes it possible for a fully loaded Boeing 747 to take off, but the airlines haven't really developed that long-distance market from Denver. Most of the international service from Denver is in the same continent—to Mexico and Canada. British Airways continues to operate, with some success, daily flights to London Heathrow Airport, and United flies the same route during the warmer months. Lufthansa has daily service to Frankfurt, and from time to time has tried regular flights to Munich from DIA. Korean Air began service to Seoul in 1997, with a stop in Los Angeles, but it abandoned the route in late 1999. In fact, Denver has the smallest proportion of intercontinental flights of any of the world's largest airports. And it's certainly large—tenth busiest in the world. City and chamber officials continue to try to get a direct, if not nonstop, airline connection between Denver and Asia.

Building a new airport had another advantage. The former airport site, with its acres and acres of abandoned runways, offered great development opportunities. The 4,900-acre plot of land on which old Stapleton Airport stood has been reconfigured into an urban planner's dream, with a mixture of residential, retail, and office development that the city calls "one of Denver's greatest community assets." A 1989 fact sheet on the new development said, "With its excellent location close to downtown and good highway and rail access, this city-owned land can generate significant revenues, create jobs and enhance surrounding neighborhoods." The site is six times as large as the Denver Tech Center on the city's southeastern edge—and, city planners note, it took the Tech Center twenty years to be fully developed.

Bob Albin gives the new airport much of the credit for attracting telecommunications companies to the Denver area—a central location with easy access to all parts of the country, and a good starting place to reach global markets. But it may also have played a role in attracting some unexpected benefits, too. In February 2008, ConocoPhillips announced it was buying the former StorageTek campus in Louisville. It was a bit of a surprise, but its economic impact is expected to be

The solar array at DIA collects enough energy to run DIA's train between the main terminal and outlying concourses. Photo courtesy of the Denver Metro Chamber of Commerce.

significant. The Houston-based energy company plans to use the 432-acre site as a corporate learning center and global hub for research and development of renewable and alternative energy "We didn't know they were coming here," said former CEO and chamber president Joe Blake. "They came here because of what they saw."

M. Doak Jacoway believes the chamber is wise to look to space science and bioscience for future growth in the area. There is still a lot of empty land around the airport; the opportunities are great. "East of the city is a natural development area for the future," Jacoway said.

"DIA sometime in the future will become a huge international hub," Albin believes, and that will enhance the Denver area's standing as a business center. And of course there's still plenty of room to expand. "Huge expansion potential," Albin said—up to 12 runways, 200 gates. "That's going to be hard for anybody to duplicate." Cities like Dallas, Kansas City, Minneapolis, Salt Lake, and St. Louis aren't able to do that. Only Denver had the huge amount of empty land available to undertake a transportation project of such remarkable size.

Even airport critic Michael Boyd conceded that "Denver has airport capacity up the wazoo. Other cities don't." But its passenger levels and prospects for international travel were oversold, he said. He believes the FAA inflated estimates for growth of passenger traffic. In 1989, Peña said the FAA was predicting 72 million passengers a year would use the Denver airport by 2000; "Denver's estimate of 61.5 million travelers is more conservative," Peña said. In fact, it took until 2008 for the number of travelers to exceed 50 million. Boyd also complained that the airport hasn't attracted new airlines—certainly nothing major since Southwest began flying out of DIA. And he was especially scornful of the claims that a new airport would allow direct flights from Denver to Tokyo and the burgeoning cities of China. "There's not an airplane flying that can get all the way to Asia" from Denver, he said, or South America, either.

But of course, Boyd added, "You can't expect any big government project to be totally pure." And, whether or not it was necessary to be so lavish in building such a grand new facility, Boyd believes it's one of the best facilities for passengers anywhere. "From a consumer point of view…it's a very efficient airport…From Bruce Baumgartner on it has become one of the most customer-friendly." Baumgartner, the former town manager of Crested Butte,

Colorado, was the airport's manager from 1998 to 2003, including during the 9/11 crisis. Wellington Webb's hiring of Baumgartner, and John Hickenlooper's hiring of Turner West to succeed him, were "high points," Boyd said; however, he felt "it was a mistake to let go of Turner West." West retired in 2008 after four years as DIA comanager or manager and twenty-two years in the Denver airport system.

Hickenlooper's office reported on its website that during West's tenure,

> DIA negotiated new agreements with Frontier and United, enabling both airlines to continue growing in Denver; opened the longest commercial runway, at 16,000 feet, in North America; welcomed Southwest Airlines back to Colorado; increased domestic and international flights, including Lufthansa's new nonstop route to Munich; opened a new 16-gate regional jet facility with 13 loading bridges; received a No. 1 customer service rating from J. D. Power and Associates, and was rated the No. 1 airport in America by Business Traveler magazine. Airport revenues increased 13 percent to $501 million, while passenger volume grew 33 percent to 47.3 million annual passengers during this period. By increasing non-airline revenues by 40 percent, DIA was able to lower airline landing fees thereby saving passengers' money and attracting more carriers.

New Hotel, Train Service

In early 2009, airport officials announced that plans to build a five-hundred-room hotel next to the terminal were back on track, and that the hotel would tie in with a new mass transit train station at DIA. Those two components, a hotel and train service, had long been promised. But even in the teeth of the 2009 recession, DIA officials sounded confident that the new facilities could be completed. Airport Manager Kim Day also said passenger traffic was expected to grow by more than 20 percent over the next decade—to something around 60 million a year. That will require building a seventh runway and at least twenty more gates on the three existing concourses. A master plan that takes the airport through 2035 also contemplates building more concourses—either D and E to the north of the existing A, B and C, or a concourse just southeast of the main terminal building. "We don't know what will happen, but we've got to stay nimble," Day told *The Denver Post*. At full build-out, with twelve runways, the airport would be capable of handling 110 million passengers and 1.2 million landings and departures a year. When and if Concourses D and E are built, the airport will have to resurrect some version of its mothballed automated baggage system, Tom Clark said.

"I don't see air travel diminishing," said airport campaign consultant Skip Spensley, despite the airlines' continuing problems with finances and fuel costs. "I think we're going to find solutions." In a prescient interview a few days before the airport opened, Bob Albin spoke to *The Washington Post* about the controversy swirling around the project: "We'll suffer through the process," Albin said. "Three years from now, five years from now or ten years from now, we'll be happy and proud of what we got."

Former mayor Federico Peña has evidence of that change of heart. He has kept this note from a converted critic, dated April 30, 2008:

Dear Mayor Peña:

I don't know how often it is that you might get "thank you" letters so long after the fact, but I feel I owe you a very sincere thank you note.

Mr. Mayor, when you were in office I did not like you at all—maybe part of it was that I just didn't like Texans—I never voted for you, I contributed small amounts of money to whomever was running against you, and then this airport thing. Good lord, why do we have to spend zillions for an airport when good ol' Stapleton was just fine?

Well, now we're well into 2008 and I felt it was high time I tell you that the airport that you built is really drop dead gorgeous—wonderful for the economy, for the people, and, though you had help it was really your doing. For whatever it may mean, I owe you a great big, honest thank you for having the vision, the drive and raw guts to keep pushing for what you believed in—even when you yourself may have had a few brief moments of question. I salute you, sir, and I wish I could personally shake your hand! Congratulations! And was it M. K. Gandhi that said (to the effect)

First they just ignore you.
Then they laugh at you.
And then they fight you...
Then? Then you win!

I hope you have a good day!

Sincerely,
Steve Sim Roberts

Denver, 1958

A November afternoon, looking west over the downtown skyline to the foothills and Mount Evans.
Photo courtesy of the Denver Public Library Western History Collection, Otto Roach, Z240.

Chapter 10

Major League

For years, Denver tried and tried to get a Major League Baseball franchise. The closest it had ever come was oil baron Marvin Davis's attempt in 1980 to buy the Oakland Athletics. But that fell through at the last minute.

Finally, in 1989—the year that Denver voters endorsed the idea of building a new airport—came an opportunity. MLB announced that it would add two franchises beginning with the 1993 season, and the public-private machinery revved up once again, as it had for the airport campaign. The Colorado General Assembly quickly passed a bill sponsored by Westminster Republican Kathi Williams creating the Colorado Baseball Commission. The commission's first executive director was longtime baseball fanatic Neil Macey of Denver Equities, and its cochairman was Larry Varnell, a Central Bank executive and former minor league ballplayer who had been involved with trying to bring big league baseball to Denver since 1977. The commission sought to strengthen Denver's bid by getting voters in the six-county Denver Metropolitan Major League Baseball Stadium District to tax themselves to build a new baseball stadium.

Aerial shot of Coors Field in 1997. Photo courtesy of John Leyba, *The Denver Post*.

The 0.1 percent sales tax—a penny on each $10 purchase—was to be used for building a new ballpark, provided MLB awarded Denver a franchise.

The election was set for August 1990, but polling that spring showed voters opposed to the tax by a 2 to 1 margin. One state legislator suggested taking the issue off the ballot rather than risk sending the wrong message and killing Denver's expansion chances for good. But baseball's supporters weren't ready to give up that easily. They pressed on with a fund-raising drive, which was struggling until Bill Daniels, Denver's cable television pioneer, donated $100,000 to the effort. It was "out of the blue," said former chamber president and CEO Joe Blake. It came "in an envelope; in the mail." That broke the logjam. "It was the jolt that saved everything," said campaign consultant Rick Reiter. Other donations soon started pouring in, and by election day on August 14, almost $500,000 had been raised.

In the early days of that campaign, before the Daniels donation, Ray Baker and John McHale came to the Greater Denver Corporation, Clark said, and asked for a loan of $50,000, money enough to do an architectural rendering. If the elections succeeded, they said, they'd pay back the loan. "This is what sold the stadium," Clark said, holding up an architects' rendition of what the new facility might look like. In fact, it turned out almost exactly the way the architect had imagined it, he said, inside and out.

"It was a very tough sell," Clark said. But after that drawing showed up on the front pages of *The Denver Post* and the *Rocky Mountain News*, "the polls flipped." A majority now favored the tax. Even so, the election—at the primary, in mid-August, at the height of the baseball season—was close. Voters in Denver and Adams County, in fact, were opposed by narrow margins. Boulder County was narrowly in favor. The more affluent suburbs in Arapahoe, Jefferson, and especially Douglas counties turned it to an overall vote of 54.3 percent in favor.

"The campaign began without a constituency," Joe Blake explained. Because the issue was referred by the legislature, not a citizen initiative, there was no built-in campaign structure backing it. It was Reiter's idea to set up an "ironing board brigade," where supporters could register their names on 3-by-5-inch index cards. The Hispanic community and sports talk shows also got enthusiastically behind it.

Reiter was recruited by Chris Paulson and Odell Barry, cochairs of the baseball campaign committee. He said the idea of the ironing boards was to create a database of voters who were favorable to the idea of paying a small tax to support baseball. "It was a huge effort," Reiter said. With it, the baseball campaign was able to identify more than 30,000 unaffiliated voters. Combining that with lists the campaign purchased of subscribers to sports-oriented magazines, the committee assembled a list of around 115,000 people to check against registered voter rolls. There was nearly a 30 percent match. "There wasn't a lot of TV [advertising]." Reiter said. "The budget went into direct mail."

Some opposition had surfaced, but it wasn't well-organized or well-funded. "There were people shooting at it all the time," Reiter said, including *Rocky Mountain News* columnist Gene Amole. But the campaign's narrowly focused voter list—plus the fact the voting was at the primary election, when turnout typically is smaller and more manageable—was enough to create the numbers needed for passage. "If it had been a general election, we probably would have lost," Reiter said. As it was, "We were able to turn out an extra margin of people" who might not have voted in the party primaries.

Clark said voters were receptive to the idea that even if they voted for the tax, they might not have to pay it—not unless Colorado actually got the franchise. "It was a no-risk deal. I want baseball, but if I don't get it, I don't have to pay for it. What am I really risking?" Clark said the credit goes to Ray Baker, chairman of the stadium district, and John McHale, chairman of the baseball committee, for crafting the question that way.

The campaign was not hugely expensive, maybe $700,000, Reiter said. There wasn't a lot of advertising; that came only toward the final days of the campaign. But there was a lot of word of mouth. Supporters spoke at service clubs and luncheons. After all, said Clark, "we didn't have any money." And after the issue passed, the chamber got back the $50,000 it had lent to get the architect's drawings made.

Step Two

The baseball campaign, though shorter and much less expensive than the campaigns for the airport, was just the first step. Tucking that bouquet of voter approval under their collective arms, baseball's local supporters began earnestly wooing MLB for an expansion franchise.

Ten days after the election, Colorado's Baseball Advisory Committee, chaired by governor Roy Romer, assigned to a new entity, the Colorado Baseball Partnership, the job of recruiting an ownership group. Romer deserves "huge credit" for mounting the postelection ownership search, Blake said. Gary Antonoff, a classmate of Blake's from East High School and Dartmouth, and Trygve Myhren, a cable television pioneer, were appointed by Romer as cochairs of the Colorado Baseball Commission Finance Committee. Their principal assignment was to help put together the franchise's ownership group.

The partnership assembled a far-flung and diverse group that was criticized by some civic leaders for having too many out-of-town members. But some of them eventually dropped out, and the early investor group included a number of local business owners, including Hensel Phelps Construction Co., Jerry McMorris's NW Transport Service Inc., Dick Monfort of the Greeley meat-packing firm, KOA Radio, the *Rocky Mountain News*, which had an $8.5 million agreement with the club, and Coors Brewing Company. Dick Robinson, former chairman of the chamber, is given much of the credit for bringing together the local investor group, and according to chamber minutes from October 1992, "The GDC worked around the clock for 10 days preparing the application in conjunction with the new owners."

Clark relates the process—the second of the two campaigns to win baseball—in a more colorful narrative. Things didn't always go optimally. The printed presentation, on slick paper, smeared in the copy machine. "This was one of the first laser printers; we chose the wrong paper. They had to send the whole thing out to New York City to get it redone...I set the application on fire over at Kinko's," Clark said. The team worked on the presentation around the clock for two straight weeks, "12 hours on, 12 hours off; this place was cluttered with Domino's [Pizza] boxes." The computers they were using were primitive by today's standards—a string of low-capacity processors "daisy-chained together." Back then, there were no simple PowerPoint programs. When it came time to do the presentation, with competitors in Florida working online as well, it was taking 90 seconds to make and save last-minute changes. Mickey Monus, who with John Antonucci was one of the original managing general partners of the ownership group, was pacing frantically. Finally, Clark said, Antonucci "screams at the top of his lungs: 'I don't wait for computers; computers wait for me!'"

Monus, startled, inadvertently kicked the plug out of the computer, and the whole system went down. By fortunate coincidence, though, the Florida system crashed at about the same time, and the Denver team was able to resurrect its presentation within the five-minute window it had been given. All the high-powered executives, not really understanding what was going on with these machines, meekly left the room while the young computer geek made things right again, Clark remembers.

Denver made it to the short list as a finalist, but there was more tension to come. When it came time for the selection team to visit the city, the locals went all out. They arranged to clear the airspace approaching Stapleton while the visitors arrived on their private jet. The local team had three helicopters waiting to show them the city, including the future site of Coors Field at Twentieth and Blake streets, where lines had been painted on the ground to show the general layout of the foul lines. Members of the baseball committee were playing softball below as the choppers passed overhead. The helicopters landed at Mile High Stadium, about a mile to the west, where the movable east stands had been pushed back to show how the field would be configured as a temporary home for baseball while the new field was being built. "We have Bob Howsam Sr. [Broncos founder] standing on the pitcher's mound, surrounded by some of the ownership group," Clark said.

Thirty minutes had been scheduled for a sales pitch, but "they're out there about 10 minutes; then they wanted to see the clubhouse." The clubhouse had been laid out as if for a game, with various jerseys, chewing tobacco, and sunflower seeds in the lockers. The clubhouse stop was supposed to take about an hour and 10 minutes, "but in 20 minutes, we're gone again." Supporters of the bid chose to interpret this as a positive sign. "We were saying, 'Well, they know we're a good baseball town; they don't need all this presentation. We got this thing.'" The expansion team and the locals boarded a bus to the governor's mansion for lunch. Wyoming's governor also was there, and a farmer from Nebraska—to reinforce the idea that people would be willing to travel long distances to see a real baseball game. "We tried to show them that distances are very different here than in a metropolitan area," Clark said.

Lunch went comparatively well, but there were problems at the next stop. Katy Feeney, the National League's vice president of media relations, had made it clear to Clark that there should be no big public displays during the selection team's visit. But after lunch, as the group pulled up to what is now the Wells Fargo Center (the "cash register" building) "You can hear this chant, 'baseball, baseball, baseball'—and you can actually see the windows moving in and out," Clark said. A large and loud crowd had gathered, at least a couple of thousand, signing a petition to show their support for baseball. Clark insists the local group knew nothing about this spontaneous, window-rattling show of support. "And Katy Feeney comes around the corner and she gives me a look that would freeze-dry coffee."

And then, as the group was moving from one level to another, one of the visiting owners was heard remarking to another, as Clark remembers it, "That was really fun. Wasn't that just a blast? Too bad we're not giving them a team." What had been a beautiful, sunny, clear day—March 26, 1991—suddenly seemed to turn gray and gloomy. "Now we thought the reason everything had gone so fast is that they just wanted to get it over with," Clark said, to "get back here and announce there's no deal."

It was about three o'clock in the afternoon; there was supposed to be an announcement from the expansion team in time for the five o'clock news. Five came and went, then 5:30, then 6—and nothing, no announcement. "We really thought we'd lost it," Clark said. Finally, at about 6:45 PM, Doug Danforth, chairman of the expansion committee, "shows up and starts talking about the advantages of local ownership. We were all wondering, where did that come from?" Clark said.

On June 10, MLB Commissioner Fay Vincent announced that Denver and Miami were the picks of the expansion committee for new National League franchises. On July 5, team owners unanimously gave their approval.

About a year later, Clark and others asked Jeff McMorris, the brother of Jerry McMorris, one of the Rockies' major partners, what had happened that afternoon in late March. What had changed the expansion committee's collective minds? McMorris explained that the local ownership partners had finally decided that Monus and Antonucci probably didn't have the money they said they did. "So," Clark said, "Jerry got in the car and drove out to Golden and sat down with Pete [Coors] and said 'These guys don't have any money and if you want to have major league baseball in this town, the local guys have to step way up.'" By "way up," he meant an investment of $30 million, in addition to the $5 million the brewer already had paid for the naming rights to Coors Field. With Charlie Monfort from the Greeley meat-packing family supporting them, they had assembled the local, family-based ownership team with the long-term reliability that MLB was looking for. "When they went up to the meeting with the baseball guys... essentially they said, 'These guys are out and we're in,'" Clark said.

Although they did business in Colorado and co-owned a vacation home in Vail, Monus and Antonucci were both from Youngstown, Ohio, a town with a reputation for organized crime. Monus was president of a drugstore chain called Phar-Mor, and Antonucci ran his family's beverage distribution business. They were never embraced wholeheartedly by Denver fans, to say the least. Monus in fact was indicted on fraud and embezzlement charges just two months before the Rockies played their first game in 1993. He eventually served ten years in a federal prison and was released in 2005, two years before the Rockies' best season to date. The Rockies had a remarkable late-season drive in 2007, winning twenty-one of their final twenty-two regular-season games. They swept through the playoffs, too, but lost four straight in the World Series to the Boston Red Sox. By then, the names Mickey Monus and John Antonucci had all but been written out of Rockies' history. Neither was even mentioned in the 2007 Colorado Rockies Information Guide.

Denver's Field of Dreams

Ground for the new Coors Field was broken at Twentieth and Blake streets in downtown Denver in September 1992. Denver clearly was ready for the big leagues. The Rockies played their first two years at Mile High Stadium while Coors Field was being built, and the team quickly started setting attendance records. Nearly 4.5 million fans attended that first season, far surpassing any other baseball team's record. Although Coors Field had almost a third fewer seats than Mile High, records continued to be set after the new venue opened at the start of the 1995 baseball season. The stadium, built of bricks and steel girders in nostalgic ballpark style, proved to be a major force in bringing a new vibrancy to downtown Denver. It was "the ultimate urban renewal project," Joe Blake said; the park "really propelled" the rehabilitation of areas that were on the edge of, if not right in the thick of, blight. "It exceeded all economic impact forecasts," said Kelly J. Brough, Blake's successor as the chamber's president and CEO.

The baseball stadium bonds were on track to be paid off early, in 2000—twelve years ahead of schedule. But because revenues were so good, Broncos owner Pat Bowlen sought to test the waters to see if voters would approve continuing the tax—to its original payoff date—and use the money to finance a new football stadium. "It was a comparatively easy sell," said Gail Klapper, who chaired the Denver Metro Chamber of Commerce the year the stadium tax passed, in 1998. In fact, the extension of the existing tax passed more comfortably than the original tax had passed eight years earlier—by 57 percent, compared with 54 percent in 1990.

A baseball or football stadium needs taxpayer support, Clark said. At indoor venues like the Pepsi Center, designed

The singing of the national anthem at the World Series at Coors Field, October 30, 2007. Photo courtesy of *The Denver Post*.

primarily for pro basketball and hockey, it's possible to make a profit by running 180 to 200 or more events a year. An outdoor stadium designed for baseball or football can't approach that number of paying customers, Clark said. "You have to pony up."

The 0.1 percent sales tax is still on the books, until 2012, but Clark said the bonds probably will be retired a year before then. "Of course there's a line of people who want to extend it for other purposes." It was easier to extend it for football, another sports-related purpose. But for another cause, like homelessness, that might be more difficult. And Clark doesn't think that's a good idea. "That would only feed the public's suspicion that you can never get rid of a tax," he said.

Former governor Bill Owens, a Republican who went against a majority of his party to support the 2005 Referendum C proposal, and who worked closely with the chamber to get that issue passed, voted against the stadium. "From a public policy standpoint, it diverted resources that really might have been better used in other ways." But still, he said, "I love where Coors Field is. I love the new football stadium...I'm kind of glad I was outvoted."

Baseball vote (1990 primary) by county

	% yes	% no
Adams	48.9	51.1
Arapahoe	61.5	38.5
Boulder	51.2	48.8
Denver	49.6	50.4
Douglas	67.0	33.0
Jefferson	56.8	43.2

Overall, baseball passed with 54.3 percent in favor. Adams County and Denver voters were narrowly against it. Douglas County voters were 2 to 1 in favor.

Football vote (1998 general) by county

	% yes	% no
Adams	59.8	40.2
Arapahoe	60.9	39.1
Boulder	46.0	54.0
Denver	53.3	46.7
Douglas	63.3	36.7
Jefferson	60.0	40.0

The idea of continuing the baseball tax to fund football had slightly more support than the original tax eight years earlier: 56.8 percent in favor to 43.2 percent against. Of the six counties affected, only Boulder voted no; Denver was the next-lowest, with a 53 percent majority in favor.

Denver, November 11, 1962
Aerial view looking northwest. Photo courtesy of the Denver Public Library
Western History Collection, Dennis S. Walla, X29147.

Chapter 11

A TABOR Timeout

Infrastructure is one thing. Policy is quite another. When voters can see what their tax money will buy, or build, they've been receptive to arguments that it's worth a little investment on their part. But when the question is strictly policy—an issue, not an edifice—they may be harder to convince. It was just such a campaign that the Denver Metro Chamber of Commerce undertook in 2005—an effort to get voters to give up the possibility of extra tax refunds for the next five or six years so that the state could spend more money on things like transportation and education.

It was, said Joe Blake, the chamber's former president and CEO, "The toughest sell by far. Ideas are tough. A project, though, you can show where it goes." The campaign for the change in tax policy, Blake said, offered "a clear continental divide of visions for the future of Colorado… it was spirited, sharp, divisive, fun."

The issue divided Republicans, unified Democrats, and had major support from the business community. Without a certain amount of bipartisanship—achieved most visibly with the support of Republican former governor Bill Owens and in the campaign's three-member steering

Governor Bill Owens speaks at a September 2003 Congressional Transportation Summit hosted by the Denver Metro Chamber of Commerce. Photo © Brett Wilhelm, Rich Clarkson & Associates.

committee—and without careful, poll-driven attention to what voters would accept as ballot language, it wouldn't have succeeded, said Tamra Ward, the chamber's senior vice president for public affairs and communications. "Sadly, there is not that kind of coalition now," Ward said. It would take "another Bill Owens type" to put it together.

It also took an unprecedented amount of spending for an off-year campaign: nearly $12 million total. The Denver Metro Chamber was the largest single contributor to the side backing the proposal to let the state keep its tax revenue instead of having to refund it. The chamber's attitude might surprise those who think of chambers of commerce as reflexively antitax. They're not. The Denver Metro Chamber and most of its counterparts around the state are on the same page. They want a pragmatic government, not an impotent one.

"A most remarkable effort," said Blake. "I don't know of another issue that required an affirmative vote that had implications of a tax increase." Blake and most of the state's opinion leaders held that it wasn't a tax increase, but that was one of the major opposition arguments, and a key issue in the campaign. Neither side of the debate could seem to grasp the other side's point of view. TABOR supporters said anytime the state gets to keep revenue that it otherwise would have to return, it's a tax increase. Referendum C supporters said it's a tax increase only if the state increases the rate of taxation, not if it keeps the money it collects from existing taxes.

That debate is typical of the controversy surrounding TABOR, which is a somewhat strained acronym for Taxpayer Bill of Rights. The amendment, longer in fact than the US Constitution's Bill of Rights, passed in 1992 and restricts the amount of revenue state and local governments can keep. Its numerous provisions have the overall intent of shrinking the size of state government even as the state economy grows. Anything that exceeds the combined rate of inflation and population growth must be returned in the form of tax refunds. Most years, there has been no TABOR refund, though most taxpayers continue to get regular refunds if they've overpaid their state income taxes. But for a five-year stretch beginning in 1996, when Coloradans were buying more and earning more and thus paying more in taxes, the state did exceed TABOR's revenue restrictions and had to give extra refunds. The net effect was to reduce the state's budgetary base for the next year, and the year after that, and the next year—until the economy slowed down a bit and the TABOR refunds stopped. This "ratchet effect" lowered the state government's budget as a percentage of the total Colorado economy and put the state in a fiscal bind.

It's not just TABOR, said Kelly J. Brough, president and CEO of the Denver Metro Chamber. Other constitutional provisions "tie your hands, too"—such as Amendment 23 of 2000, which requires annual increases in public school spending that exceed the level demanded by TABOR. Or the legislature's own Gallagher Amendment of 1982, which has the effect of constantly lowering the rate of residential property tax while increasing taxes on commercial and industrial properties. The constitution has been manipulated by both the right and left sides of the political spectrum with the net result that the Colorado legislature has less fiscal flexibility than its counterparts in other states.

No one wanted to eliminate the part of TABOR that requires voters to approve any increase in tax rates, Brough said. Other states have some restrictions on their legislature's ability to raise taxes, but Colorado is the only one where the legislature simply cannot increase a tax rate without voter approval. It can reduce taxes, however—and has—and it also has interpreted the law to mean that it can raise fees and repeal exemptions, which it also has done.

"Remarkable" Coalition

The coalition-building for referendums C and D is "one of the most remarkable things ever," Blake said. The two referendums were proposed in the Colorado General Assembly, which was struggling to find enough money to fund the services citizens demanded. Referendum C in particular was a policy change, Referendum D a bonding authorization for infrastructure improvements. But if voters were going to approve a change in a rather arcane funding formula, the idea would need the same sort of broad and diverse coalition of supporters as did the campaign to build DIA, which by now had become a useful model for other campaigns.

The author of the TABOR amendment, Douglas Bruce, is an attorney from Colorado Springs, a former prosecuting attorney who had relocated from California and brought with him a decidedly unfriendly attitude toward taxation and government spending. TABOR was his third try to restrict government fiscal activity; two previous attempts—as well as half a dozen other citizen initiatives from other tax activists—had failed since 1966. TABOR passed with 53.7 of the vote in 1992, the highest-turnout election in Colorado's history, driven in no small part by Ross Perot's independent campaign for president.

Referendum C effectively eliminated the worst of TABOR's government-shrinking provisions and, until 2011, let the state spend money it was collecting from taxes already in place. Referendum D, which didn't pass, would have established some specific priorities for how to spend that unrefunded money.

It had become clear that TABOR was hurting state government's efforts to provide services demanded by its citizens. The "ratchet effect" essentially imposed an annual reduction in the state government's share of the state's economy, and it was starting to bind. Public-policy leaders were worried; changes had been under discussion for a couple of years. The chamber had worked on a 2004 initiative that went nowhere because the principals "were all going in different directions," Blake said. Entrepreneur Rutt Bridges's Bighorn Center had spent more than a year touring the state in an effort to show voters what kind of a bind TABOR and other conflicting constitutional amendments were creating, but that 2003–04 effort didn't lead specifically to a ballot issue, either.

In 2004, the Republicans still controlled the House and Senate, and if TABOR was going to be fiddled with, the Republicans wanted something to be done, too, about the school-funding requirements in Amendment 23, a 2000 constitutional change that required annual increases in spending that clearly conflicted with TABOR's limits. But the Democrats won a majority in both chambers in the 2004 elections, and that changed the dynamic. Democrats were more pro-23 and anti-TABOR. The chamber agreed as the 2005 legislative session got underway to do polling to see what voters would accept in the way of a remedy to this fiscal Gordian knot. "A lot of careful thinking" went into the ballot language, Blake said.

The committee running the campaign to seek a remedy, Coloradans for Responsible Reform, filed articles of incorporation on March 23, 2005. It was a bipartisan group. Democrat Rick Reiter was the campaign's director. Walt Klein, mastermind of several Republican election victories, was the election strategist; David Hill, whose firm has a bipartisan list of clients, was the pollster; and Katy Atkinson, a middle-of-the-road Republican, was the spokeswoman. The Denver Metro Chamber of Commerce, through the Metro Denver EDC, made the first campaign donation of $250,000. The campaign's slogan was Move Colorado Forward, and there were "thousands of yard signs," said Tamra Ward, the chamber's senior vice president for public affairs and communications. The chamber eventually contributed more than $700,000 and "a great deal of time, too," she said.

Unlike the projects the chamber had backed up until then, "it was an idea rather than a toy," Blake said. And, while it deeply split the Republican Party, the largely Republican chamber threw its weight behind it, as did a few Republicans who had been struggling with TABOR's fiscal straitjacket, including, most notably, then governor Bill Owens.

Governor Bill Owens

"I was involved in writing it, getting it through the legislature and on the ballot," said Owens, who had until then enjoyed a reputation as a fierce fiscal conservative. "I strongly supported what came out of the process, and I have to applaud the chamber as well. The change was essential to the operation of government."

Owens took a battering from his own party. Only a handful of moderate Republicans in the legislature lent their support. "It was as bitter an intraparty fight as I can recall in some time and exposed fault lines that may not be instantly repaired," political consultant Eric Sondermann said. Owens had voted for TABOR in 1992, and he remains a strong supporter of the basic idea—not just voting on taxes, but putting some restraints on state government spending. However, he adds, "We had an obligation to fix the impact of the ratchet." There had been a 16 percent reduction in actual state revenue during the 2001–02 period; the base from which each year's permissible growth is figured had shrunk to unsustainable levels. That was the ratchet effect, and it was shrinking the state government's ability to keep up with citizen demands. But with Referendum C, "when revenues come back, we're allowed to get back up to where we started," Owens said.

The former governor doesn't support permanent changes to TABOR. With the "ratchet" fixed, he said, TABOR's draconian revenue limits probably won't be triggered again. "I will be a significant opponent to changing TABOR if it's not backed up by facts and a reduction of new spending initiatives," Owens said.

In a letter to "fellow Coloradans" during the campaign for the change, Owens wrote that he believes TABOR "has prevented us from going down the tax-and-spend path that has damaged other states, most notably California." Owens had to be careful to preserve his conservative credentials, but he also had to govern a state that had seen serious cuts in higher education and transportation. And there continue to be those who insist it was a tax increase. As Owens pointed out in his letter, "Over the past several years, I have cut roughly $1 billion in state spending…But we have cut what we can responsibly cut…Even by playing catch-up, we will have a smaller government than we would have had. That's hardly a radical expansion of government." He said some of the critics of the timeout were exaggerating what the fix would do. "Some who share my strong support of TABOR clearly overreacted," he said.

Campaign director Rick Reiter said that the "legitimate bipartisanship" of the campaign involved more than Owens. Former Republican US Senator Hank Brown was a major supporter and spokesman. The three men who chaired the campaign committee were two Republicans—Joe Blake and Bruce Benson—and a Democrat, former Colorado State University president Al Yates. Reiter said it showed that "you could be a good Republican and support TABOR and still be for the referendum."

There were two other factors that helped convince voters to vote for the measure, Reiter said. One was the severity of the state's fiscal situation—higher education, in particular, was one of the few areas not subject to constitutional fiscal restrictions, and it lost its comparative share of state funding so other needs could be met. The other was that the proposed correction came from the legislature, where it had been tested and improved by debate, giving it credibility; citizen initiatives usually come from a group with a particular interest, all sharing the same point of view.

"Colorado was at a point where it was in need. It shouldn't have been that hard a sell," Reiter said. But it wasn't easy. The hardest argument to overcome was that people would be giving up annual tax refunds for five years—even though by far the majority of the refunds state taxpayers were receiving weren't because of TABOR. That argument was offset, though, by "the sheer weight of people saying this is something we have to do." Even the conservative editorial board of *The* (Colorado Springs) *Gazette* "had to acknowledge" the need for the amendment, Reiter said.

The Campaign

In the legislature, the proposed correction was contained in House Bill 1194, the "Colorado Economic Recovery Act." It included both Referendum C, which asked voters to forgo their TABOR refunds for five years, and Referendum D, spelling out some $2 billion in financing: $1.7 billion for transportation, mostly roads and bridges; $146 million for school construction and maintenance; $50 million for higher education facilities; and $175 million for fire and police pensions. The final votes in both chambers were strongly in favor: 46 to 19 in the House and 26 to 9 in the Senate.

The two referendums did not attempt to dismantle TABOR, Tamra Ward points out; they worked within its provisions. It was "not an attack" on the amendment; it used the instruments that TABOR provided. "For the first time, and perhaps the last, 1,200 organizations pulled in the same direction," she said. The effort would be difficult to duplicate today. "We can't cookie-cutter this campaign," she said. The bipartisan committee of Blake, Benson, and Yates met weekly to talk about funding. Owens was heavily involved, as were his budget chief Henry Sobanet and policy advisor Chris Castilian. Ward said Owens didn't really have to be talked into helping the campaign. It was something he wanted. Proponents of the changes were, Ward said, "squeaky clean about our reporting." They didn't want to give opponents any ammunition to challenge where they were getting their support.

In December 2004, the chamber hired David Hill's firm for a total of $100,000 and launched a statewide poll on what voters might accept. There were rounds of "shuttle diplomacy," Ward said, as the results of public opinion polling were presented separately to Governor Owens and leaders of the legislature. The language of the referendum, as it finally was drafted, was guided by the results of that polling. Voters wanted things in accessible language: for example, *roads* polled better than *highways*, Ward said. And an "endless time out" from TABOR, as incoming house speaker Andrew Romanoff had suggested—coupled with a small reduction in the state income tax—"wasn't going to work."

Turnout for the off-year election in November 2004 was slightly less than half the eligible voters—a small number, for Colorado. The margins of difference were small. Referendum C passed by 52.1 percent to 47.9 percent.

Referendum D failed, with 49.4 percent in favor to 50.6 percent against.

Proponents outspent opponents by about $8 million to $3.6 million. The Denver Metro Chamber of Commerce was the biggest single contributor to the pro campaign, at $708,000. Two Democrats were next on the list: Pat Stryker at $280,000 and Ted Gill at $250,000. The Colorado Education Association kicked in $250,000, and two other major unions added $240,000. There, too, was evidence of the bipartisan nature of the campaign seeking a reprieve from TABOR's more onerous provisions.

The campaign "couldn't have been done without Owens," Blake said. "The logistics of this thing were unique." There was no party structure behind it, although Democratic legislators widely favored it and Republican legislators were split. The chamber, though, was "unified, supportive, energetic, focused" for an eleven-month campaign in which "all resources were directed at this campaign," Blake said. It was necessary to "connect emotionally" with a broad constituency—the disabled community, nonprofits and churches, people who were being hurt by the continued paring down of government services. The breadth of support was extraordinary, with city councils in both liberal Boulder and conservative Colorado Springs passing resolutions of support. "You had to convince people to give up a small amount for the future, for a vision of Colorado," Blake said.

In an analysis immediately after the November 1, 2005, election, political consultant Eric Sondermann concluded that the results had more to do with socio-economic factors than politics or ideology. Left-leaning Denver and Boulder counties were 60 percent or more in favor of Referendum C, but heavily Democratic Adams County was nearly 58 percent against it. In heavily conservative counties, such as El Paso and Douglas, Referendum C still did better than it did in Adams—it didn't pass, but it got favorable votes of 47 to 48 percent. Sondermann's take on the thirty thousand swing voters who said yes to C but no to D was that they felt committing to long-term debt was not a good way to get out of a fiscal crisis; plus, the wording on D was "far longer and more convoluted and off-putting" than C's comparatively simple language.

Reiter noted that Referendum D did better in Republican-leaning counties but lost in the larger counties that lean Democratic. "The Democrats didn't get behind it," he said. "They favored mass transit projects but roads, not so much."

"There was not a day we didn't think we'd win," Ward said. But the loss of Referendum D was a deep disappointment; "it hurts to this day. Maybe people were confused." It may have been that D was not given enough political vetting, she said. Its language was more legalistic, possibly more difficult for voters to understand.

More Issues to Defeat

In the 2008 elections, the chamber was in more of a defensive posture, fighting against initiatives that were seen as antibusiness, and—in a tradeoff with labor—also fighting an attempt to impose right to work (RTW) requirements that make it harder for unions to organize. That was a difficult choice, a rebuke to the stance that probusiness organizations like chambers of commerce are expected to take. It was "unfathomable," Ward said, but the Denver Metro Chamber did oppose the RTW initiative. Only two people on the chamber's board of directors opposed that position. And even the US Chamber of Commerce "said they get it," she said. Under the circumstances, it was a justifiable position for the Denver Metro Chamber to take. Its members include the pipefitters union. It partnered with labor to fight three more initiatives on the 2010 ballot that would further diminish the state government's flexibility to deal with fiscal problems. "What we agree on is it's all about jobs," Ward said.

The Denver Metro Chamber put defeating those three new fiscal initiatives at the top of its political agenda for 2010. Amendments 60 and 61 and Proposition 101 were all designed to further cut government taxes, spending, and borrowing. They were offered by activists who either don't believe that the state's hodgepodge of conflicting fiscal amendments has put Colorado at a disadvantage, or they simply wanted to see government cut even further. They lost decisively, however, getting favorable vote margins of 25, 27, and 32 percent in the November general election.

This history of fiscal initiatives collectively has restricted the legislature's budgeting flexibility to the point that valued services are suffering. Forty years ago, higher education represented about 20 percent of the state's overall budget. Now it's about 7 or 8 percent. Higher education has been losing ground because it's about the largest pot of money that isn't constrained in some way by constitutional provisions. It's a fiscal rat's nest, with new restrictions—or new requirements on how to spend money—always a possibility. The unpredictability created by Colorado's wide-open initiative process "drives the business community nuts," Tom Clark said. He quoted an unnamed colleague in the economic development game who told him, "I've been telling all my clients to stay away from Colorado. We're convinced that through your initiative process you're systematically dismantling higher ed."

Clark said it makes him wonder sometimes if Coloradans have a collective suicidal streak. "I mean, we live in this incredible place, very little scandal politically; politics, up until recently, has been played with a small 'd' and a small 'r', we work really hard at not screwing it up, we cleaned up the air…we've built an incredible center city, we've rewritten history in America for center cities, we're part of the urban renaissance, we have this extraordinary internationally known playground outside our door… and then we sit down and decide to just kill ourselves, kill our economy."

Denver, 1990–2000

View of the glass-and-steel Tabor Center (named for H.A.W. Tabor, gold rush legend of the 1800s) and the Sixteenth Street Mall. Photo courtesy of the Denver Public Library Western History Collection, Roger Whitacre, X-29147.

Chapter 12

Models for the Future

Founded in the heady days of the gold rush, tested by cycles of boom and bust, this once-isolated region at the eastern edge of the Rockies has prospered because its people have learned to work together. The campaign for DIA is a major example of how the business community can collaborate with the public sector to promote projects that add exponentially to a metropolitan area's quality of life and prospects for the future. But there are plenty of others—not just concrete and steel, but ideas, too. "You build a sense of ability," said Tom Clark. "An outstanding public psyche emerged from that: We can do this."

The airport, said Kelly J. Brough, president and CEO of the chamber since October 2009, "is the perfect example" of a "game-changing investment." Virtually all of the project's early critics have been won over, she said. "I don't think you could pick a better example" of how what may have struck some as a "crazy investment" turned out to have a tremendous positive impact. "It was the smartest, most critical economic decision Mayor Peña and business leaders made years ago. At this time, at this moment, we should be highlighting it all over the place."

It takes a bipartisan effort, said Bruce Benson, the former state Republican chairman who now heads the University of Colorado system. And it takes active support from the business community. "They step up to the plate," said Benson. "Our business community is about as engaged as any business community in the United States."

About $10 billion was invested in various infrastructure projects over one ten-year period, former chamber CEO Joe Blake said. And much of it came to a head in 1995. The airport opened in February. Cherry Creek shopping center opened in August. Coors Field opened for the new baseball season in April. The new central Denver Public Library opened in March. The new Elitch Gardens opened in the Platte Valley in May. The first light-rail line, a demonstration project barely five miles long, had opened in October 1994. All of this happened after TABOR took effect, so every one of those projects required voters to approve; every vote had a campaign, and every campaign needed money, which "overwhelmingly came from the business community," Blake said. Businesses have been consistently engaged and have shown "a unique and positive relationship to the shared vision going forward." Despite the inconvenience, that's one good thing that comes from voting on tax-supported projects; voters

The Denver skyline as seen from Elitch Gardens. Photo © 2011 Greg Thow.

believe they have a buy-in. "You ought to vote on tax increases for this very reason," Blake said.

And, because Denver doesn't have a lot of corporate headquarters, "these are people who had to ask permission" to contribute their time and their companies' money to the various campaigns. (Blake's father, in fact, worked for Mountain States Telephone and Telegraph, later Qwest, which now has joined the list of headquarters that have left for other places.) Business people also were important in assessing the financial and sometimes technological feasibility of these dream projects: FasTracks, the light-rail system, is an example. The heady days of billion-dollar-a-year civic improvements may have slowed, Blake said, but the leadership has stayed together. "The same individuals are called on today."

Every five years or so, said John Frew, who masterminded the campaign for voter approval of the airport, an issue comes along that requires the kind of political-business partnership that worked on the airport campaign. The Scientific and Cultural Facilities District is another example, or bonds for improving public amenities, or a sports facility. Or the loosening of the state's fiscal straitjacket. "I'd hate to see where we'd be if we didn't do those things," Frew said.

Frew remembers going to a meeting in Governor Romer's office early in the airport campaign. All of the principals were there. "Look out the window," the governor said, and they did. From the governor's office on Capitol Hill, the view stretches across three blocks of public parkland to the spire of the City and County Building, and beyond it, 14,260-foot Mount Evans. To the north are the skyscrapers of downtown Denver. To the south, the architectural eye-grabbers of the Denver Art Museum and Denver Public Library. It was "grand planning" and then innovative view-protection easements that preserved that vista, Romer told the group assembled in his office, and that's how airport planners should be thinking. "That caught everyone's attention," Frew said. "Let's just do this right."

Urban affairs critic Neal Peirce thought they did get it right. In a May 26, 1989, speech to the Greater Denver Chamber of Commerce, just ten days after the second successful airport election, Peirce said, "It's a great pleasure to visit a city that has its act together."

Peirce's theme was that the city should proceed with a quality airport design. Most critics thought it did. A July 1993 article in *Buildings* magazine said the new airport would be a "city-defining landmark…expressing both the mountains and the vast open spaces." The roof at DIA, the magazine said, "will certainly achieve the goal of bringing travelers a memorable experience, bringing a majestic landmark to the city, and taking airport patrons—from generations to come—to new heights in air travel."

There was negative criticism, too, continuing for months, even years, after the new airport opened. But the critics eventually were marginalized by the airport's performance and growth. Although they were critical of the level of spending on the airport—"fistfuls of money thrown in a multitude of directions"—Paul Dempsey and the other two University of Denver professors who published a 1997 book on DIA did find something good to say about the process. Or, rather, they found Airport Director Jim DeLong, and he said something good. The frenzy was inevitable, DeLong told them. "He makes two points," Dempsey et al report:

> First, in order to build a new airport, it was necessary to build a political coalition of business, the media, labor and minority interests, to succeed in the public referenda on the issue. The votes in Adams County and Denver were crucial in defusing the small groups of highly motivated anti-growth and pro-environmental individuals, which in so many other cities have derailed such projects. The two votes in favor of DIA made stopping it infinitely more difficult. But the quid pro quo would be that each of these constituencies—business, labor, minorities and the press—would expect either to have a piece of the action or (in the press's case) to have the latitude to make recommendations and have them endorsed. In other words, DIA could not have been built without rewarding the political constituencies that had supported it. And the most amazing thing about DIA, in DeLong's view, is that, given the inability of any other city to build a new airport in two decades, DIA was built at all.

DeLong's second point was that "while Peña was cast as the visionary who imagined a great airport and sold it to the people, he handed the ball off to his successor, Wellington Webb, to build it. It is significantly more difficult and less glamorous to complete a megaproject than it is to begin it."

A Model for Winning Elections

Dick Fleming believes the Greater Denver Corporation, created in economically difficult times to promote the airport and other improvements, is a blueprint for what needs to be kept in mind as the region copes with whatever the future might bring. "The overriding message is: We have a crisis; the business community needs to step up and deal with the political community. But they don't want to do it unless the region stops squabbling and starts cooperating." The challenge was "to figure out a way to make real this notion of how we work as a region as opposed to all these fiefdoms."

And it has been noticed. *The New York Times*, in a January 6, 2009, article about "high anxiety" in the real estate business, called attention to the Denver area's potential for riding out the recessionary storm. It quoted Randy Nichols, president of Denver's Nichols Partnership, whose remarks at a meeting of real estate developers, it said, "had a curiously calming effect.

It isn't that Denver expects to avoid rough economic seas, but there is a sense that leaders here have constructed an ark on which to weather just such a storm.

A number of elements are cited as keeping this region afloat as other areas founder: investments in public transportation, aggressive economic development and, most significant, a two-decade campaign to diversify the region's economic base from oil and gas to alternative energy, aerospace, technology and telecommunications.

The *Times* article continued:

The Urban Land Institute and PriceWaterhouseCoopers, in a report titled 'Emerging Trends in Real Estate 2009,' listed Denver among 15 American cities expected to outperform the rest of the country. The report cites a good balance in housing supply and demand, a strong federal and state government presence to support jobs, continued population growth and a widely diverse economy.

Colorado's governor, Bill Ritter Jr., has pushed for investments in renewable energy to build on the presence of the Department of Energy's National Renewable Energy Laboratory at Golden, Colo., about 12 miles west of downtown Denver. A broader research initiative through the newly created Colorado Renewable Energy Collaboratory, which combines statewide university researchers with those at the national laboratory, has helped create a reputation for Colorado as 'a new world leader' in solar, wind and biofuel research, said the Collaboratory's executive director, David Hiller.

Such efforts have already attracted a Danish wind-turbine manufacturer,

Vestas. It is building turbine blades at a plant in Windsor, Colo., 58 miles north of Denver, and has plans for two more plants that will employ hundreds.

Governor Bill Ritter (left), at the National Wind Technology Center near Boulder, flips a ceremonial switch with Dan Arvizu (middle) and Barry Nicholls (right). Photo courtesy of DOE/NREL, Siemens.

The battle plans from the DIA campaign already have been used in winning regional elections to construct new arenas for baseball and then football. And not just in winning at the polls, but in convincing the state legislature to refer the issues to voters. These were "really the son of the DIA plan," said M. Doak Jacoway, 2001–02 chairman of the Denver Metro Chamber. Jacoway said it's important to study how advances have been made in the past, "so we don't have to reinvent the wheel each time."

The airport campaign, Bob Albin said, was a chance for the business community "to get heavily involved in a project most people never get involved with…to really see a successful public-private project." The Denver Corporation for Economic Development raised $8 million from businesses for the two airport campaigns. "The city would never have been able to do that," Albin said. "It was a project of the City and County of Denver but undoubtedly would never have been successful without the full support of the business community…It was truly a successful public-private venture of gigantic size and scope." And, he added, "It's remarkable for how fast it happened; 16 years start to finish—that's just a miracle."

A ballot issue, such as the airport, or the arenas, or multimodal transportation, will pass "if the stars are in alignment and there's some benefit to it," Frew said. Proponents need to tell the voters what the problem is and what can be done to solve it. "You have to strike when it's high in people's minds," he said. Town meetings are crucial. "We had hundreds of town meetings" on the airport project. "Identify questions, answer them—prepare for them. That way, by the time the advertising starts, most people have made up their minds."

It's important to "tell stories" to voters to help them make sense of globalization and other economic trends, said Susan E. Clarke, a professor at the University of Colorado at Boulder. Not tall tales, but anecdotes that illustrate how a project makes sense for a region's economic health. Clarke, who was speaking in Denver at the National League of Cities Forum on Economic Vitality, said local leaders make a difference by engaging stakeholder groups and citizens in a process of developing an overarching economic strategy. The strategy must make sense in terms of the community's history, its assets, and its goals—its "story." Articulating this story publicly and persuasively is a key role for leaders, she said.

Another strategy, if you have the right people for it, is to involve that increasingly rare creature, a popular public figure. Former governor Roy Romer's personal approach helped win the necessary votes in Adams County to annex land for DIA. He stepped in because Mayor Peña wasn't popular in Denver's northern suburbs. In fact, until John Hickenlooper came along, it would have been difficult for any Denver mayor to get any votes in an Adams County popularity contest. "It was a tough campaign," Romer said. "The thing I was gambling on is it would just convey the importance of this [project] to the state of Colorado…It wasn't just 'fat cat

Denver' taking advantage again…I was doing this because I had more acceptability than any mayor of Denver."

DIA's Potential

Former mayor Peña, now back in Denver as a senior advisor for Vestar Capital Partners, said perhaps the airport's greatest continuing advantage for the future is its tremendous potential for expansion. "That was the point" of building it, he said. Adams County said the airport has been a success for them, too. And more is yet to come, including a hotel at the airport and access by rail. "It will happen. It will be even better," Peña believes. "This airport would not have been built without the chamber's active involvement," he said. And it was "the first major demonstration that we can work regionally." "We signed a peace treaty," Peña said—so cities in the

An artist rendering showing the proposed hotel and light-rail additions to DIA. Photo provided courtesy of Denver International Airport.

region wouldn't be competing against each other for the same plum projects.

The region's voters for years after the airport and other project approvals continued to be in an expansive mode—generous to a fault, some critics would say. Bond issues for infrastructure improvements continued at an accelerated rate well into John Hickenlooper's administration, as did voters' willingness to approve what they were told was investing in the future. In November 2008, Denver voters approved all eleven of the mayor's ambitious proposals—a total of $500 million for 215 projects ranging from prosaic street paving to new libraries and a new symphony hall.

Former chamber chairwoman Gail Klapper agrees. Voters have been "extraordinarily generous…They have come to understand that building things that people like to use—especially in difficult times—really works." Because voters approved these projects, she said, "people got jobs, and these are lasting amenities." The political climate, though, is getting increasingly negative. "I worry about our ability to make the same case today," Klapper said. "People have hunkered down in their own sphere."

Klapper, director of the Colorado Forum, a statewide bipartisan coalition of business and private interests, headed the Denver Metro Chamber in 1998, the year voters approved extending the baseball tax to build a football stadium. "There clearly was initial opposition to all of these"—the stadiums, FasTracks, especially DIA. Despite some "nuanced differences," in all of these campaigns, "it was the same argument, to promote the idea of investment at a time investment was difficult." And there was a similar strategy, Klapper said: "The work before the work made the ultimate controversy seem less so." The difference is that, as she reflected on spending $10 billion in ten years, "in today's world, it doesn't seem expensive at all."

Former governor Bill Owens, a Republican, thinks it's fair to call these government stimulus projects. And he thinks in some cases "it's a fair criticism" that the chamber "has a predisposition toward spending initiatives." His assessment of the chamber's philosophy is that "there's a role for government and a role for infrastructure." He said he has benefited from that, in getting the chamber's support on initiatives he supported. But he also believes that the chamber definitely favors government projects more than opposes them. The chamber, Owens said, "seems to operate on the premise that any project providing jobs is in the chamber's interest. It

Denver mayor (prior to becoming Colorado governor) John Hickenlooper. Photo courtesy of the Denver Metro Denver Chamber of Commerce.

doesn't recognize that some of these may diminish jobs elsewhere."

Tamra Ward said that aspect of the Denver Metro Chamber surprises some people. They believe it's all about being pro-business, but there is much more than that, she said. "We're very pragmatic...We wear not a partisan hat but a business hat. What it means is that somebody's always mad at us."

A Continuing Concern with TABOR

Most members of the Denver Metro Chamber of Commerce favor further fixes to TABOR. Simply continuing Referendum C does no good, Tamra Ward said, because there's no money. The key is to see, through polling, what Coloradans will accept. "Trust your instruments," she said, and trust your polls to tell you what will work. As it did in the 2008 campaigns to defeat right to work requirements and what the chamber called "poison pill" initiatives that would have threatened the viability of Colorado businesses, the chamber partnered with labor again in 2010 to fight three petition issues on the ballot that would have further restricted the state's ability to address fiscal problems

"We're already polling on this," Ward said in the spring of that election year, to find out what voters want, and what they might accept as reasonable alternatives. Polling, she said, provides invaluable information about who needs to be won over, and what to say to them. When you think about it, she said, the chamber really needs to concern itself more with ballot issues than it does with which particular term-limited politicians are elected to their eight-year stints upon the stage of public policy. "Politicians come and go," Ward said, "but organizations like this live on."

One of the many provisions of TABOR is that governments can't spend money on ballot issues, which makes it even more critical that private interests—the business community—raise money to support the good ballot initiatives and fight the bad ones. And, too, there was some concern in the business community that Governor Ritter had not been as skilled a politician as either Roy Romer, the Democrat who helped get the airport built, or Bill Owens, the Republican who disappointed his conservative base by supporting referendums C and D. Ritter's approval ratings *were* lower than those of his predecessors, suggesting that his leadership on issues that could improve governance is not as highly regarded by the public.

Also, Ritter's best bipartisan instincts were thwarted by single-party rule; some Democrats in the legislature saw no reason not to try to enact as much of their party platform as they could get away with, and it put the governor in a spot. While the political parties might like it, it's always more difficult for those outside government when one party controls the governor's office and both house of the legislature. Ward, a veteran of lobbying that lawmaking body, agrees. Ritter surprised most of Colorado's political observers when, citing family concerns, he chose not to run for a second term in 2010. That made him the first governor since 1974 to serve only a single term, and the only one in decades longer to bow out voluntarily. He was succeeded by the popular Denver mayor John Hickenlooper, who will have the disadvantage—or advantage—of working with a legislature under split party control.

Government Accountability

Lobbying has a bad reputation. But real life is loaded with lobbyists, including a lot of well-intentioned people who have something they want to get done—or undone. They ask their elected representatives to help them. That, in its purest essence, is lobbying. But when so much of the elected representatives' flexibility to manage finances has been removed at the ballot box, "it doesn't allow you to hold elected officials responsible," Kelly J. Brough said. "I think what people want is more confidence that they know where things are going."

The legislature's diminished power to budget with any flexibility is an ongoing problem in the state's governance. Higher education continues to be underfunded, thanks to conflicting ballot issues that direct money to other favored areas or force a portion of tax collections to be returned to taxpayers. The very process by which such restrictions come into existence is also of concern to the chamber. The comparative ease of amending Colorado's constitution makes collaborative governing more difficult than in other states, where the legislatures have more power, and the chamber has from time to time expressed interest in reforming the initiative process.

"In Colorado—maybe it's a work ethic—I understand people's desire to vote on things, especially finances," Brough said. "We really have to honor that and respect it." And yet, she said, the unpredictability of what voters might choose to do next to the state's fiscal policies hurts efforts to recruit business. "The initiative process creates uncertainty," she said, and businesses looking for places to expand or relocate don't like uncertainty.

Looking west toward downtown Denver from City Park. Photo © 2011 Willie Gibson.

She is among the many who think Colorado needs to make it more difficult to amend its constitution. Only about half the states even provide for a citizen initiative—a petition to put changes in the law before voters for their approval or disapproval. Colorado is one of only fifteen that provide that access to either the state constitution or the statute books. And Colorado doesn't differentiate—the same number of petition signatures will put either a constitutional amendment or a statutory change on the ballot, and a simple majority will pass either. The number of petition signatures is among the lowest anywhere. So most advocates opt for amending the constitution, because it's harder for the legislature to change the language. Lawmakers can amend a statute, but they can't just pass an amendment to the constitution; voters have to approve it, too.

"We need a higher threshold" for amending the constitution, Brough said. Colorado Concern, Club 20, and a number of business-oriented organizations concerned about public policy, mostly close to the political center regardless of which way they tend in partisanship, have been talking about changes for years. But it's not an easy sell politically. The chamber's polls have shown that the public favors easy ballot access by almost the same wide margin that community leaders, public and private, think it's a bad idea. "We're probably all arriving at the same conclusion that something needs to be done," Brough said. "What do we want as Coloradans and what makes sense?"

Colorado is among the top three states for ballot issues. Oregon and California are right up there, too, but in 2008, with fourteen ballot issues, Colorado outdid them all. Few of those issues passed, however, which could be seen as a positive sign in a state where petitioners' pet peeves often become law. Voters have been "sending a message but to the wrong address," Tom Clark said, punishing the legislature for the sins of Congress. Today's angry voters might have a hard time believing it, but the Colorado legislature actually has a history of repealing tax increases once their purpose is accomplished. Clark said he believes that voters are not simply tax averse. The right question, with the proviso that you don't pay it if you don't get what you want, will pass—as it did in the baseball stadium tax.

Bob Albin calls the ease with which special interest groups may place controversial issues on the ballot "one of the biggest challenges facing Colorado's electorate." Ideally, voters would take the time to understand these often-complex issues. But the ideal is the exception. Albin said the business community tries to explain its side of these controversies, but it requires "large sums of money to fight nuisance, or dangerous legislation that properly should be debated and resolved by the state legislature rather than by a statewide vote."

The chamber's top priority for 2010 was to defeat the latest round of damaging ballot initiatives, Clark said. "The real priorities for us are educational achievement and a permanent source of public funding; our universities have gone from great to very good…major employers are saying they're kind of satisfied with research universities. 'Kind of'; that's really scary."

Voters are smart, Clark said. They aren't knee-jerk antitax. Political name-calling, though, "keeps you from ever having that type of civil discussion. And that's what drives the business community nuts." They want more predictability. "Literally, businesses' lives have been at risk," he said. The chamber did support a legislative referendum in 2008 that would have raised the signature threshold for petitions to amend the Colorado Constitution and lowered the number of signatures for statutory changes. But Referendum O, as it was called, failed by 4 percentage points. Clark said if the chamber hadn't been so absorbed in defeating the anti-business "poison pills," it would have put more money and effort into Referendum O.

Initiatives force business to spend a lot of time playing defense, Joe Blake said. "I worked on at least two campaigns, maybe three, to defeat some of Doug Bruce's stuff."

Clark mused, semi-seriously, that it may be time to turn the tables on the antitax activist. "Doug Bruce is just dropping $250,000 and just keeping us constantly playing defense," he said. So, Clark suggested, why not just repeal Amendment X, Section 20, (the TABOR amendment) and replace it with just the simple vote-on-taxes requirement? That's what people thought they were voting for, anyway—not all those other revenue-shrinking, government-restricting provisions. "What you do is put Bruce on the defensive. Every year; just keep on doing it like he kept doing it."

Keeping It Together

Several of the community leaders interviewed for this book are concerned that the spirit of community, the regionalism that put turf wars aside, may be losing momentum. Economic stress, they say, can create urgency for greater regional cooperation, or the competition for scarce dollars can tear at the fabric of regionalism. In 2010, disagreement had surfaced over the FasTracks light-rail transit system. The Denver Metro Chamber continued to support light-rail expansion, but some of the communities that worked together in 2004 to make FasTracks happen worried they wouldn't get the lines they were promised.

Supporters of the system, including the chamber, were trying to get the federal transit funding requirements re-drafted so that the local commitment to the system is given more weight—such as the $4.7 billion approved by Denver-area voters—and not just population density, which the East has but the Denver region doesn't.

"We've got to finish FasTracks." Promises need to be kept. A new Veterans

Denver skyline and gardens in Civic Center Park, August 2006. Photo courtesy of Jerry Cleveland, *The Denver Post*.

Administration healthcare facility—originally a clinic, now planned as a $1 billion hospital—is a selling point for rail service, Clark said, and needs to be part of the federal budget. The hospital, at the University of Colorado's new Anschutz medical campus in Aurora, would be a logical light-rail stop.

Clark's biggest fear is that the carefully assembled coalitions that worked together for the airport, the sports stadiums, the other bond issues, and the relief from TABOR might become consolidated under a self-appointed leader who wants to control "and people will forget how to work together." The key is to diversify, he said, to push power out to as many people and as many places as possible. Command and control doesn't work, he said. Leadership must be collaborative—and trusting. People, he said, do aspire to higher ethical behavior, "but they worry that others won't."

Joe Blake isn't sure that people today would be as generous as they have been in the past. Those heady days of the late twentieth century were "a unique period…like a quarter century of abundant moisture" after years of drought. "We were very proud of ourselves because of those campaigns." He cites a favorite quote from a literary figure (whose name escapes him) who said, "In times of prosperity, merit is obscured; in times of adversity, merit is revealed." The Denver region, the Front Range, the Rockies, went through that time of adversity and challenged it with projects that have proven to have lasting value. "We have seen the results of a persistent vision," Blake said. "That's a couple of generations when you think about it. If you get people with shared, persistent vision…over time they will achieve it."

Denver at 150

Denver celebrated its 150th birthday on November 18, 2008.

Photo courtesy of Reza A. Marvashti, *The Denver Post*.

Chapter 13

Lessons Learned

By Bob Albin

The Denver Metro Chamber of Commerce, as the oldest and largest business organization in Colorado, is frequently called upon to take a leadership role in community issues because it represents such a large and broad spectrum of the region's employment base.

When the chamber is confronted with such issues, the process of determining a "chamber position" reaches well into its membership. Various committees, task forces, and the board of directors meet to hammer out an appropriate response based upon the interests of its membership and the region's business climate in general. Once a position is determined, the chamber, through its staff and volunteers, becomes a public advocate for its point of view.

If the chamber's position supports a need for new or increased taxes to fund the issue or improvement, the chamber attempts to articulate the cost or benefit of its position. Does approving the measure enhance the business climate and save or create jobs? Seldom has the chamber taken a position supporting something designed purely to stimulate the local economy. Rather, the organization tends to favor those initiatives that support business growth or attract new business to the area, such as a new airport, educational needs, cultural facilities, or other amenities required to attract or sustain businesses. Because of its business bias, the chamber is generally seen as promoting business growth rather than as an advocate for stimulus spending.

The Denver Metro Chamber has served as the primary spokesman and advocate for the region's business community for well over a hundred years, making it a credible voice on matters that affect the business climate in Colorado. Occasionally, the chamber becomes involved in matters that are generally political or governmental in nature. A ready example is the chamber's role in the planning and construction of Denver International Airport in the 1980s and '90s. In 1978 the chamber's board of directors initiated the discussion about the airport when it formed a committee of Colorado business executives to evaluate the useful life remaining for Stapleton International Airport, a facility owned and operated by the city and county of Denver and opened in 1929.

A yearlong study conducted by this committee concluded that Stapleton was nearing its capacity and would need major expansion or replacement by the turn of the century, some twenty year hence. This report ignited regional interest in the issue and quickly led to a FAA/Denver-funded site selection study that was to be managed by the Denver Regional Council of Governments. Although this four-year study recommended expanding the current airport onto the adjacent Rocky Mountain Arsenal grounds, neighboring communities in Adams County, where the arsenal was located, strongly opposed such a move, creating a stalemate. The chamber became the catalyst for negotiating a compromise with Adams County business leaders that ultimately located a new airport facility east of the arsenal in another part of Adams County.

Denver and Adams counties promptly signed between them an agreement for the new site, yet the chamber still proved indispensable in rallying support in the ensuing two popular votes that finally made construction possible. The chamber created a new entity, the Greater Denver Corporation, raised over $8 million, and used the proceeds to help sell the airport project to the community through ads, research, information packets, speakers' bureaus, and get-out-the-vote efforts.

Why was the chamber's participation so critical and effective? Colorado's economy was struggling in the 1980s, and the business community as well as the city and state were looking for ways to stimulate business growth. The chamber determined that transportation was, and would be, an essential component of Colorado's economic vitality, and the Denver airport played the most important role in the transportation of people and goods in the region. Without a vibrant airport, Colorado's economy would surely suffer. This issue proved to transcend politics, and leaders from both sides of the political aisle as well as business and labor leaders came together to support the project. The new airport was seen as an integral part of the region's appeal to new and existing businesses. A key strategy of the airport plan was that no new taxes were used to build the facility since it was funded by revenue bonds and proceeds from airline ticket taxes that comprise the existing federal Airport and Airways Trust Fund, an entity designed for such aviation needs.

The airport project spawned enormous job creation and helped assure Colorado's economic viability into the coming century, all funded by users of the new airport. The effort to approve the airport proved to be a successful public-private partnership that gained broad approval because it solidified Denver's position as a major aviation hub without an increase in taxes.

Robert L. Albin chaired the blue-ribbon committee that did the pioneering planning for Denver International Airport (one admirer said it should have been called "Albin International") and chaired the Denver Metro Chamber of Commerce (then the Greater Denver Chamber of Commerce) in 1991–1992.

By Tom Clark

If you read the history of Denver, you note that the business community's role in the region's progress is mentioned only in passing. Oh, yes, you'll see references to the colorful industrial icons of the nineteenth century—the Tabors, Boettchers, the Browns, etc. But otherwise, the history of metro Denver is painted largely on the faces of its politicians. The typical line in some history book said, "Mayor So and So brought great prosperity to Denver...and the business community helped."

There's a reason why the dominant role played by business and the chamber over the past 150 years is often absent in history's annals. Quite simply, writers don't know many businesspeople. If you are a reporter *cum* author, you certainly don't come out of the business section of *The Denver Post* and you certainly don't hang with corporate executives. What you're writing about, or want to be writing about, is politics, not economics.

For twenty-five years I've sat at the knees of our modern-day business icons. In most respects they are more responsible for driving this community to its eminent status than the politicians who have come and gone.

Who cooked up the idea that maybe we should build a new airport? It was the manager of Delta Airlines' station at Stapleton Airport who first suggested it during a chamber retreat in 1972. Three chamber members were appointed to the "Airport Committee." One was the famous builder of the Denver Tech Center, George Wallace. Another was Bob Albin, a small-business leader who eventually chaired the chamber. But Albin's greatest contribution was his continuous DIA involvement starting in 1972 and stretching to the airport's opening and beyond. He chaired the Airport Planning Committee and worked with three mayors, three governors, and four airport managers. A year after DIA's completion, Bob Albin was the only person still involved at DIA who was present at the beginning.

The entire election to annex fifty-four square miles of Adams County into the City and County of Denver was financed by the business community through the chamber's affiliate, the Greater Denver Corporation, and business and political leaders in Adams County. The construction of DIA left undeserved scars on lots of business leaders. Vilified personally in the media, accused of money laundering, dragged through IRS audits, attorneys general investigations, and ultimately vindicated in a trial, business leaders in this community never faltered. They knew that Colorado could not survive without a world-class airport. They put their reputations on the line for the good of the community.

In the 1980s, when Denver's air quality was killing its ability to attract new jobs, it was the chamber that championed the "Brown Cloud Study" to determine the sources of our poor air. The chamber then made an unpopular decision, calling for universal emissions testing for all cars. Thanks to that courageous stance, metro Denver has enjoyed almost two decades of clean air.

When Colorado finally got its shot at major league baseball, the legislature created the Colorado Baseball Commission and directed it to conduct a sales tax election for a new stadium. Trouble was, the General Assembly didn't give the commission a dime. The polls were running against the whole idea when two businessmen, Ray Baker and John McHale (volunteers without pay), asked the Greater Denver Corporation board for a $50,000 loan to complete some architectural renderings of the stadium. When the renderings hit the front page of the *Rocky* and the *Post*, the polls turned up and more money flowed from businesspeople like Bill Daniels. The rest, as they say, is history.

Invesco Field is another example. While verbal jousting ensued over whether there should be a roof atop the new stadium, the Broncos were busy taking the D off their helmets, just in case Los Angeles wanted an NFL team. Again, it was the business community that put together and funded the campaign that allowed the excess revenues generated during the Coors Field construction to be spent on Invesco Field at Mile High. The Broncos stayed. The role of the business community in the creation of FasTracks, the Convention Center, and virtually every major economic event in metro Denver came from the continued and sustained political and financial support from a politically savvy and enlightened business community.

The work of diversifying the region's economy from its oil, gas, and defense concentrations in the 1960s to the modern, exciting community we now all share was not always driven by politicians. Certainly they helped. But in the long run it was the continuing, sustained leadership by the business community, working together with elected officials, that crafted the vision of this community. Moving from an insular, inward-looking "good old boys" club of the '40s and '50s, the chamber has diversified its leadership and changed forever its role in the community.

Tom Clark is executive vice president of the Metro Denver Economic Development Corporation and the Denver Metro Chamber of Commerce. He was the founder and first president of the Metro Denver Network, the Metro Denver region's first economic development program.

By John Frew

Jack Swigert didn't live long enough to vote in the airport elections, but his spirit played a role in their success. After endless studies and numerous attempts to solve so many challenges with Stapleton, the proponents had a problem.

The need to replace an outdated, poorly functioning airport coupled with a stagnant economy provided the right ingredients and timing for this enormous public works project. This wasn't about bricks and mortar—for many it was about survival. It followed the civic efforts to build the railroads, the Moffat Tunnel, and the trans-mountain diversions of earlier eras. It was so big, so important that it gave people something to believe in, a goal they could understand. I am proud to say that we created an environment where anyone and everyone could participate.

We had our champions in Roy Romer, Federico Peña, Steve Cramer, Leo Younger, and Harold Kite. But Stapleton would still be Denver's airport had it not been for the thousands of people who volunteered to do whatever it took to convince at least 50 percent of the voters that we were right. People of all ages knocked on doors, made calls, delivered yard signs, and answered every objection posed.

Early in the effort, we hired the best political professionals from both parties, and they created a speakers college to train an army of advocates to answer all objections at countless forums. The theory was to have fellow citizens debate the issues, rather than the paid professionals. It was a smart move, because even the best TV commercials could not have anticipated the arguments that we encountered.

Here are a few of my favorites: (1) Opponents in Adams County gained traction with the rumor that the fifty square miles of DIA would have to be leveled rather than just the roads, runways, and buildings, and that the spoils would be dumped in Commerce City. Their fliers screamed, "What will they do with the dirt?"; (2) Early in the campaign, 12 percent of Adams County voters were opposed out of fear that it would be named after Federico Peña (to his everlasting credit, Mayor Peña sidestepped the issue and endorsed DIA as its name, and to the city council's everlasting credit, they later named the access road in his honor); and (3) At the outset of a debate at a high school gym overflowing with opponents, long-time community leader Hal Shroyer admonished us never to use yellow paper for our fliers because it implied an evil intent on the part of the opponents (honest, we simply ran out of white paper).

The last may be my favorite because it was Hal who led the effort to have a statue of his friend and former Colorado congressman, the late Jack Swigert, placed in the US Capitol. Each state is allowed one statue in the Capitol building of a leader whose lifelong leadership reflects most favorably on the state. I disagreed with Hal on the airport but not on his goal to have Jack Swigert represent Colorado in the US Capitol. As is customary, an exact replica of that statute is placed somewhere in the sponsoring state. Ours is located at DIA. I love that statue because it reminds me of an undefeatable attitude.

The Colorado economy of the mid-1980s was a lot like the flight of Apollo 13, on which Swigert was a crew member. Both ended well after a focused effort to recover. Let's hope it's not the last time we try something monumental.

There's a rhythm to every campaign: from the initial excitement through the evolution of issues and then to a period when voters' focus and emotions kick in and the choice is made. You can usually calculate these things with a candidate, but gaining voter approval for a controversial public project is a crapshoot. With DIA, the outcome was always in doubt, but failure was never an option.

John Frew was the lead strategist in the campaigns to get Adams County and Denver voters to endorse Denver's plans for a new airport. Frew, a lawyer, also was former senator Tim Wirth's chief of staff and counsel to the authority that brought the Rockies to Colorado.

By M. Doak Jacoway

Since its inception in 1884, the Denver Metro Chamber of Commerce has been seen as a powerful and visionary force for the improvement of the Denver metro area and the state of Colorado as a whole. Denver's citizenry over the years has come to respect the chamber's community advocacy and its balanced views regarding perceived community needs. As a result of this earned respect embraced by the larger Denver community, when the chamber has spoken, the community has listened. To illustrate the point, there are three recent, prime examples of how the chamber's vision and leadership have influenced the electorate to support community-based projects with taxpayer money.

In 1989 the Denver community approved for a second time the issuance of revenue bonds to finance the construction of DIA. To this day, the airport's construction was the most ambitious aviation project in US history. When the airport opened in 1995, Denver citizens realized they had approved the funding of an economic-generating crown jewel that allowed bondholders to be paid back on a schedule more accelerated than originally anticipated.

In 1997, the Denver Broncos won its first Super Bowl Championship, and in November 1998, Denver voters were asked to approve the extension of a Denver seat tax to help fund the construction of a new football stadium. Once again, the Denver citizenry, led by the chamber endorsement, allowed for the funding of the much-needed new facility and were rewarded by a second consecutive Super Bowl Championship.

Finally, by way of illustration, in 1999 Denver voters approved taxpayer funding for a significant road expansion through the heart of the Denver metro area. This project became known as T-REX (TRansportation EXpansion). The project was completed on time and under the $1.8 billion projected budget.

In each of the three examples, taxpayer funding was approved largely due to the credibility of the chamber's endorsement. As a result of the success of the aforementioned and numerous other projects, the chamber's advocacy and resulting credibility has allowed Denver voters to feel comfortable in approving taxpayer funding for community improvement projects.

M. Doak Jacoway is president of Jacoway Financial Corporation, a company he formed in April 1987. He was chairman of the Denver Metro Chamber of Commerce in 2001–2002, and he is the motivating influence behind this book.

By Maureen McDonald

Since 1974, leaders have been nurtured and developed through the programs of what is now known as the Denver Metro Chamber Leadership Foundation. The leadership foundation serves primarily private-sector professionals who wish to understand the region's issues better, with a goal of deepening their civic engagement. This series of opportunities helps level the playing field for anyone who wants to work hard and get involved. Rob Cohen, a successful entrepreneur who eventually chaired the chamber and leadership foundation boards and has made significant impact in both youth mentoring and bringing sporting events to Denver, reflects on his start in the Mile High City:

> When I first moved to Denver and was starting a business here, I became part of the Leadership Denver class of 1991. The invaluable perspective I gained on the metro region and the relationships I built were the springboard for the growth of my business and civic engagement, including my work with the Metro Denver Sports Commission, the I Have a Dream Foundation, the Leadership Foundation and the DMCC.

Today, Cohen is chairman and CEO of IMA Financial.

One of the ways the business community continues to churn out inspired and engaged leaders is by developing a shared vision of what the region can become. The vision work has many roots, and one is the fact that metro Denverites are willing to take a hard look at their communities and work together to discover solutions to complex, thorny problems. The more than two thousand alumni of the Denver Metro Chamber Leadership Foundation's programs have not only studied our region carefully, but many have participated in annual trips to other parts of the United States, Canada, and Mexico to compare and benchmark our progress. Former leadership foundation chair Jerome Davis, a regional vice president at Xcel Energy, offers this perspective:

> The Leadership Foundation's work is very simple. They inspire community trusteeship. The people that participate care about the future of our region and want to become involved in making their communities better and more effective.

The inclusiveness of the conversation and the act of studying others' perspectives are part of what contribute to a shared vision that will withstand stress. That's why I am optimistic about the emerging leaders who are eager to learn about and support a healthy community. Over the past decade, the leadership foundation has grown to include programs that serve a continuum of needs, from collegiate through retirement. Our alumni include the most effective leaders of the region in the private, public, and nonprofit sectors, and we are fortunate to be part of a business community where people deeply care about the health of the region and forming mutually respectful working relationships between the sectors.

Maureen McDonald is executive director of the Denver Metro Chamber Leadership Foundation.

Tamra J. Ward

After more than a decade with the Denver Metro Chamber, I can confidently say three things about the impact this organization has had on Colorado: elected officials work hard to understand the perspective of the business community and what matters to us; the chamber brings the business community together to fight and support legislation and initiatives that make a difference to Colorado's business climate; and the chamber continues to focus on businesses of all sizes, from one employee to ten thousand employees, to ensure that public policy helps them do what they do best—innovate and grow.

The Denver Metro Chamber has a history of working closely with Colorado's elected officials, whether they are our congressional delegation, our state elected officials, or local elected people. For nearly 150 years we have worked with, cajoled, supported, pressured, and, in the early days, bribed our elected officials to steer their concentration toward the business community. For the most part, we have been successful. In recent years, we have elevated our presence at the national level with a second national convention, and the thoughtful nature of Colorado has turned our state into a recognized political bellwether for the nation.

We have been fortunate enough to be the often-sought-after partner for the sitting governor, regardless of political party, and are seen as a valuable advocate by state legislators—all while never taking sides in candidate elections. This organization's impact will be felt for generations to come, because we look at the long view and work for public policy that will not just change the future, but create a better one.

One of the challenges as an advocate for business is understanding the intersection between business, government, and the economy. Business provides the taxes (payroll, property, and corporate) and the jobs that are the engine driving Colorado economy. We rely on government to provide us with a quality education system, a well-maintained and efficient transportation system, and reliable infrastructure to enable our businesses to be successful. Preserving the delicate balance between taxes, regulation, and service provision—Colorado's business climate—is our primary mission. No organization has the data expertise, the resources, and the history like the chamber does to successfully carry out this goal. We have been doing it for nearly 150 years, and I expect we will do it for 150 more.

Tamra J. Ward is the senior vice president of public affairs and communications for the Denver Metro Chamber of Commerce.

Denver Metro Chamber of Commerce Board Chairs

R. W. Woodbury 1884–1887
E. M. Ashley 1887–1888
Donald Fletcher 1888–1889
H. B. Chamberlin 1889–1890
I. B. Porter 1890–1891
H. A. W. Tabor 1891–1892
S. H. Elbert 1892–1893
William N. Byers 1893–1895
F. W. Crocker 1895–1896
H. P. Steele 1896–1897
Edward Monash 1897–1898
J. F. Campion 1898–1900
William N. Byers 1900–1901
Charles F. Wilson 1901–1902
R. H. Malone 1902–1903
Meyer Friedman 1903–1904
J. F. Callbreath, Jr. 1904–1905
J. S. Temple 1905–1906
A. J. Spengel 1906–1907
Meyer Friedman 1907–1908
E. L. Scholtz 1908–1909
F. L. Bartlett 1909–1911
C. A. Johnson 1911–1912
Allison Stocker 1912–1913
E. J. Yetter 1913–1914
T. B. Stearns 1914–1917
Cass. E. Herrington 1917–1918
F. L. MacFarland 1918–1920
William V. Hodges 1920–1921
I. I. Hoak 1921–1922
Roblin H. Davis 1922–1923
Elias M. Ammons 1923–1924
L. Ward Bannister 1924–1926
R. M. Crane 1926–1927
Fred Farrar 1927–1928
Tyson S. Dines 1928–1929
Herbert S. Sands 1929–1932
Adolph F. Zang 1932–1933
William E. Russell 1933–1934
C. A. Shinn 1934–1935
J. Harry Custance 1935–1936
Stanley T. Wallbank 1936–1938
Henry C. Van Schaack 1938–1939
R. J. Osenbaugh 1939–1941
John C. Davis 1941–1942
A. J. Bromfield 1942–1944
Charles O. Voigt 1943–1946
R. S. McIlvaine 1946–1948
Benjamin C. Essig 1948–1950
Frank J. Johns 1950–1952
Askel Nielsen 1952–1954

Walter K. Koch 1954–1956
Arthur L. Baldwin........................... 1956–1958
Clair G. Henderson 1958–1959
John C. Davis, III 1959–1961
Robert T. Person 1961–1962
Roy L. Mason 1962–1963
Roger D. Knight, Jr. 1963–1965
Theron L. Arckerman 1965–1966
Rollin D. Barnard 1966–1967
James O. Hickman 1967–1968
Edward F. Kingman 1968–1969
Ralph J. Becker 1969–1970
John. E. Fuller................................. 1970–1971
Shelby F. Harper 1971–1972
Bruce M. Rockwell.......................... 1972–1973
William D. Johnson 1973–1974
Donald E. Jansen............................ 1974–1975
Theodore E. Brown 1975–1976
Richard L. Deane............................ 1976–1978
A. B. "Pete" Slaybaugh 1978–1979
John D. Hershner........................... 1979–1980
Lael S. DeMuth.............................. 1980–1981
Dick Walker................................... 1981–1982
Donald Hoffman............................ 1982–1983
Ralph Cox 1983–1984
Jim Baldwin................................... 1984–1985
Richard A. "Dick" Kirk 1986–1987
Bill Walters 1987–1988
Roger Ogden.................................. 1988–1989
D. D. "Del" Hock............................ 1989–1990
Richard L. "Dick" Robinson........... 1990–1991
Robert "Bob" Albin 1991–1992
Barbara B. Grogan 1992–1993
Charles Steinbrueck 1993–1994
Lawrence A. "Larry" Atler 1994–1995
Dave Wollard.................................. 1995–1996
John Scully 1996–1997
Gail Klapper 1997–1998
David E. Bailey 1998–1999
Douglas "Doug" L. Jones 1999–2000
Harry T. Lewis Jr. 2000–2001
Cathey M. Finlon 2002–2003
Don Kortz....................................... 2003–2004
Ned Minor...................................... 2004–2005
Tom Honig 2005–2006
Rob Cohen 2006–2007
John Ikard 2007–2008
Madeline "Mimi" Roberson 2008–2009
Charles "Chuck" Ward................... 2009–2010
William "Bill" N. Lindsay III........... 2010–2011
Hassan A. Salem 2011–2012

Bibliography

Allard, Wayne. *Colorado United States Senators*. Golden, CO: Fulcrum Publishing, 2007.

Amole, Gene. *Morning*. Denver: Denver Publishing, 1983.

Barnes, Craig. *Growing Up True*. Golden, CO: Fulcrum Publishing, 2001.

Baron, Robert C. *Pioneers and Plodders: The American Entrepreneurial Spirit*. Golden, CO: Fulcrum Publishing, 2004.

Clarkson, Rich, and Robert Baron. *Colorado Rockies: The Inaugural Season*. Golden, CO: Fulcrum Publishing, 1993.

Connor, Mary Kay. *Dick Connor Remembered*. Golden, CO: Fulcrum Publishing, 1995.

Dunning, John. *Denver*. New York: Times Books, 1980.

Ferril, Thomas. *Thomas Hornsby Ferril and the American West*. Golden, CO: Fulcrum Publishing, 1996.

Fowler, Gene. *Timberline*. New York: Blue Ribbon Books, 1933.

Gunther, John. *Inside U.S.A.* New York: Harper and Brothers, 1947.

Hornby, Bill. "Eye on the Horizon." Denver: Denver Chamber of Commerce, 1995.

Johnson, Kirk. *Crusin the Fossil Freeway*. Golden, CO: Fulcrum Publishing, 2007.

Kreck, Dick. *Denver In Flames*. Golden, CO: Fulcrum Publishing, 2000.

Miller, Jeff. *Stapleton International Airport: The First Fifty Years*. Boulder, CO: Pruett, 1983.

Noel, Thomas, and Stephen J. Leonard. *Denver: Mining Camp to Metropolis*. Niwot: Univ. of Colorado Press, 1990.

Perry, Phyllis J. *A Kid's Look at Colorado*. Golden, CO: Fulcrum Publishing, 2004.

Platt, Corrine, and Meredith Ogilby. *Voices of the American West*. Golden, CO: Fulcrum Publishing, 2009.

Rocky Mountain News. *A Dozen on Denver*. Golden, CO: Fulcrum Publishing, 2009.

Smith, Duane, and Richard D. Lamm. *Pioneers and Politicians: Colorado Governors in Profile*. Golden, CO: Fulcrum Publishing, 2008. Dedication